Spoon by Annie Morris + Jonny Shimmin

First published in 2016 by Hardie Grant Books

Hardie Grant Books (UK)
52–54 Southwark Street
London SE1 1UN
hardiegrant.co.uk

Hardie Grant Books (Australia)
Ground Floor, Building 1
658 Church Street
Melbourne, VIC 3121
hardiegrant.com.au

British Library Cataloguing-in-Publication Data. A catalogue record for this book is available from the British Library.

ISBN: 978-1-78488-055-2

Publisher: Kate Pollard
Commissioning Editor: Kajal Mistry
Editorial Assistant: Hannah Roberts
Photographer: Jacqui Melville
Cover and Internal Design: Clare Skeats
Propping: Ginger Whisk
Copy Editor: Charlotte Coleman-Smith
Proofreading: Kate Wanwimolruk
Indexer: Cathy Heath

Colour Reproduction by p2d

Printed and bound in China by 1010

10 9 8 7 6 5 4 3 2 1

SPOON

—

Simple and nourishing breakfast bowls
that can be enjoyed any time of day

Annie Morris + Jonny Shimmin

hardie grant books

CONTENTS

____

6   INTRODUCTION

16   BUILD YOUR OWN BOWL

23   GRANOLA

43   MUESLI

57   PORRIDGE

75   BIRCHER

89   SAVOURY

105   SMOOTHIES

117   BREAKFAST
       ACCOMPANIMENTS

138   ABOUT THE AUTHORS

138   THANK YOU

140   CONTRIBUTORS + SUPPLIERS

141   INDEX

INTRODUCTION

———

THE SPOON START-UP STORY

Like with many start-up stories, Spoon Cereals began from a passion, in my case a borderline obsession, with breakfast cereal. Luckily I was addicted to the healthier ranges of cereals, including muesli and granola.

At work, my old creative partner learnt pretty quickly not to launch into conversation until I'd had my morning fix – a fresh bowl of muesli and granola, often mixed together with fresh fruit and a thick dollop of yoghurt or a splash of milk, all washed down with a strong cup of coffee. This resulted in an energised and happy me in the morning. It was this passion that ignited my idea for a place that other hungry and grumpy commuters could pick up a fresh and healthy breakfast bowl on their way to work and enjoy 'al desko'. The concept that had been stewing in my head at the time was London's first breakfast cereal pop-up.

Due to the way the market for a healthy breakfast was heading, I knew that others would have similar ideas, so it didn't take too much thinking time before I decided to quit my job in advertising and launch Spoon Cereals at a small food fair in south-west London. A month or so beforehand, it was at a family barbeque that I shared my idea with Jonny, who like me was looking for a new adventure in life and was keen to enter into the food start-up world. Jonny would soon become not only my business partner but my brother-in-law too...
Annie

When we first started out making cereals in 2013, the thought that someday we would be supplying retailers nationwide seemed a pipe dream: it was a concept that we wanted to test.

For the first market we attended, we prepared our granolas in the small kitchen of my London flat. We had built up to our first outing as Spoon Cereals by testing our granolas on friends and family and asking them for their favourite recipes, which we tweaked until we had something we knew was delicious and different. That first day selling at Barnes food fair in south-west London was great fun and we got some amazing feedback. More importantly, we sold out of granola and there was a lot of interest from a whole host of people, including a local shop, which later became our very first stockist.

Suitably encouraged by our first foray into the world of food, we continued to trade at several markets all over London, from the river at Richmond to St Paul's cathedral. We offered fresh bowls of cereals with a variety of yoghurts, milks, compotes and other toppings, along with bags of our homemade granola for customers to take home with them. It soon became clear that there was an opportunity to establish ourselves as a manufacturer, selling to local stores in the first instance. Our first kitchen was a shared space, but as things started to get busier we soon moved into our own space. It was tiring work, as we were doing it all – from buying ingredients and cooking to packaging and selling. We would start just after 4 a.m. and drive to the kitchen to pick up supplies before heading to a market to set up our stall. We would sell all day and then head back to the kitchen to bake more granola, sort out our online and shop orders and pack everything up for the next day. It was a grind but we both really enjoyed it.

Things started to feel surreal when we had a call from BBC Television inviting us to audition for their prime time investment programme *Dragons' Den*. We had assumed that our application had gone unnoticed, but now found ourselves pitching to the 'Dragons', high-profile investors who were going to help take our business to the next level. After securing investment, we are now established on shop shelves all over the UK and couldn't be more excited for the future.
Jonny

OUR VALUES

KEEPING THINGS SIMPLE

In this fast-paced, digital age that's full of distractions, keeping things simple is something we value very highly. Simplicity flows through everything we do: the ingredients we use, the way we make our granola, how we present it on the shelves and the way we run our business. It also defines how we aspire to go about our day-to-day lives.

Living simply for us starts with breakfast; a comforting bowl of granola, muesli or porridge. With the growing trends of brunch and healthy eating that we see developing, 'breakfast' as we know it is often enjoyed at any time of the day.

The greatest pleasures in life are often the most simple. We look forward to long, drawn-out brunches with family and friends on the weekends, as much as the quick oat porridge topped with our favourite fruit, nut or seed toppings before rushing off to work. There's something rewarding about enjoying a Bircher muesli that has been carefully prepared the night before a busy day. And we just as happily tuck into a perfectly sweet breakfast bowl as a healthy dessert in the evenings or as a nutritious late-night snack before we head to bed.

OUR MISSION

———

Giving everyone a good reason to jump out of bed in the morning.

In a literal sense, our mission statement is about putting some excitement back into breakfast time with our range of recipes and products. We want to give people something to look forward to before they go to bed during the week. Even if it means eating on the go or after the kids have been dropped off at school – we believe your morning meal should be appreciated and just the way you like it.

Our mission also reflects why we decided to start our own business. We've learned that it's certainly not easy. Realising a vision means making sacrifices and demands the support of your loved ones. Without our passion for what we do we would not have come across half the opportunities that have come our way, and certainly wouldn't have been able to publish this book and share our enthusiasm with a wider audience.

WHY WE USE MAPLE SYRUP

There are many types of sugars and sweeteners available to buy these days and refined white sugar has recently been demonised as being part of the cause of our growing health issues.

We've learned a lot from our customers and the most striking feedback we received was that the product must taste great. So when it came to choosing which sweetener to use for our granolas, maple syrup was a clear winner for its rich, luxurious and distinctive taste, as well as the minerals it contains. Although we love maple syrup as a sweetener, it can easily be substituted in most of our recipes with honey or other syrups such as date or agave.

Jonny's familiarity with this ingredient comes from his Canadian roots. He has fond memories as a child paying visits to his uncle in Ontario, who now makes his own maple syrup. Recently, Jonny spoke to his uncle, who offered to share his story of making maple syrup. We hope that this helps you to understand why we love it so much and why using a good, natural product really helps our granolas taste so special.

'Making my own maple syrup was something I always had in my mind as I was growing up. Living in an area surrounded by trees and having parents who were naturalists and heated our home with firewood probably influenced me more than I realised at the time. When I was around 50 years old, I had the urge to purchase a log home. I found one with 25 acres of hardwood trees, situated in a rural area of the Madawaska Highlands around two hours northeast of Ottawa. The previous owners had made maple syrup every year and I was determined to follow in their footsteps.

Maple syrup is produced by drilling a three-inch hole in a maple tree, collecting the sap which drips out and concentrating the sap by around forty times by evaporation and filtering the concentrate through wool into bottles. The sap collection period takes place during March and early April in my area, while the ground is still covered with snow. The sap flow is very dependent on the weather and temperature, and having three or four good sap collection days in a row is about the best you can hope for before the weather changes

and the trees shut down for a while. From my experience, the sap flows best
when night temperature is just below freezing and the following day is sunny
with the temperature around 5–10°C (40–50°F). I learned quickly that when
the sun is shining and the tree trunks are exposed to the sun, the sap flow is
best. It is a lovely experience to be in the bush on a quiet sunny day and all you
can hear is the plinking of the sap dripping into the collection bottles.

   I only produce syrup for personal use and to give away to friends and
family. It is very labour-intensive and the propane and pots I use for
evaporation are expensive, but I love making it. It is a wonderful way to leave
winter behind and welcome the warmer spring weather. One very satisfying
moment was when I was able to bring a few bottles of syrup over to England
about eight years ago for Jonny and his family to try out. You can imagine
how happy I was when I heard recently that he was going to incorporate it
into his Spoon Cereals recipes. I am waiting for the day when I can buy Spoon
Cereals in Canada and I have a feeling that it just might happen!'

ABOUT THIS BOOK

This book is the result of all our experimentation with breakfast cereals over the last few years. We focus on creating recipes that are naturally tasty and simple, using good-quality ingredients. We share our own morning creations as well as those from the creative community that we have worked with or been inspired by along the way. From independent shop owners and ceramic artists to online bloggers, food writers and chefs, so many people have had their part to play in our story.

When creating our own recipes, we often look to the seasons and use seasonal ingredients. This has been an important aspect of the business as we started by trading at markets alongside fantastic regional produce.

This book is a collection of bowl-based breakfast recipes that we enjoy eating alone or with family and friends, at any time of the day.

HOW TO USE

We want you to enjoy this book in whichever way you please, whether dipping in and out for reference when in need of inspiration or to tweak and refine to your own taste.

In this book there are breakfast bowls for a variety of occasions, with different types of bowls forming each category of the book, making them easy to find when time is not on your side.

Our aim is to provide you with a source of recipes that feel 'doable'. We hope the book won't just look pretty sat on a coffee table or kitchen cabinet but that it welcomes the occasional coffee stain and can be enjoyed by the whole household. Many recipes are designed to make hectic weekday mornings a bit more bearable: granolas (pages 25–40) can be made in large batches and stored in a clip top jar and Birchers (pages 77–87) made leisurely the night before.

Oven temperatures: If you are using a fan-assisted oven, please reduce the oven temperatures in the recipes by 20°c (36°f).

BUILD YOUR OWN BOWL

Breakfast is something that we all enjoy in our own special way. Our picky tendencies tend to shine through at this time of day, and for a lot of people routine is important. Perhaps it's to do with the fact that we are breaking the overnight fast and so our bodies crave certain foods. For this reason, we have created a section of the book that allows you to build your own bowl (pages 16–21) to suit your needs and tastes.

The format of the 'build your own bowl' section reflects our first-ever trading day with Spoon Cereals, which consisted of a market stall table full of various locally sourced ingredients, homemade flavoured yoghurts and fresh fruit toppings, inviting all our customers to create their own perfect bowl.

We hope that this section will speak to those of you who are feeling a little tired of your breakfast rituals and, perhaps, are looking for variety in your morning routine. We want to give you the confidence and freedom to do what you do best in the morning, so we've suggested ingredient ideas that we've discovered throughout our (extensive) breakfast research. Soon, it won't be long before you'll be dreaming up breakfast bowl recipes of your own.

BUILD YOUR OWN BOWL

——————

We all have our own morning rituals, including how we enjoy breakfast. The great thing about our pop-ups and events was finding ourselves deep in conversation with other breakfast enthusiasts, who all had their own favourite bowl-building techniques! We thought that we might help some of you break out of your own routine by suggesting a few combinations that can work well together and inspire you to experiment with your own ideas. We hope you enjoy creating your own bowl.

BIRCHER

CHOOSE YOUR GRAIN

RYE · OATS · SPELT · GF {MILLET · QUINOA} GF

ADD FRUITS

FRESH

Chopped apple

Blueberries

Raspberries

Apricots

DRIED

Sultanas

Figs

Cranberries

Apricots

ADD CHIA SEEDS (optional)

LIQUIDS

MILKS/YOGHURTS

Almond

Dairy

Coconut

EXTRA FLAVOUR/SWEETNESS

Apple juice

Lemon juice

Vanilla extract

Maple syrup

SOAK OVERNIGHT

TOPPINGS

NUTS · SEEDS · FRESH FRUIT · NUT BUTTERS

PORRIDGE

CHOOSE YOUR GRAIN

OAT RYE SPELT GF {MILLET QUINOA} GF

ADD YOUR LIQUID

WATER DAIRY MILK ALMOND MILK COCONUT MILK

ADD YOUR FLAVOUR

SWEET
Ground cinnamon + Maple

SAVOURY
Ground cinnamon
Ground turmeric
Ground ginger

FRUITY
Blueberry + Banana

VEGGIE
Grated carrot + Mixed spice

COOK FOR 10–20 MINUTES

TOPPINGS

NUTS SEEDS FRESH FRUIT NUT BUTTERS

GRANOLA

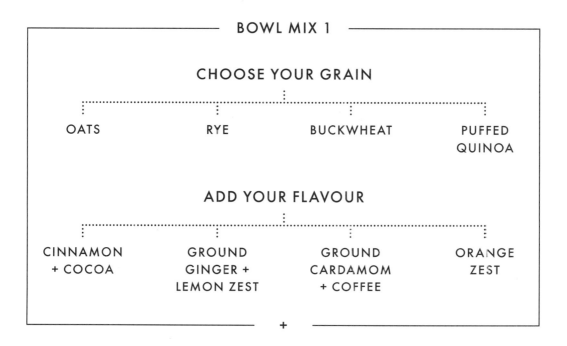

BOWL MIX 1

CHOOSE YOUR GRAIN

| OATS | RYE | BUCKWHEAT | PUFFED QUINOA |

ADD YOUR FLAVOUR

| CINNAMON + COCOA | GROUND GINGER + LEMON ZEST | GROUND CARDAMOM + COFFEE | ORANGE ZEST |

+

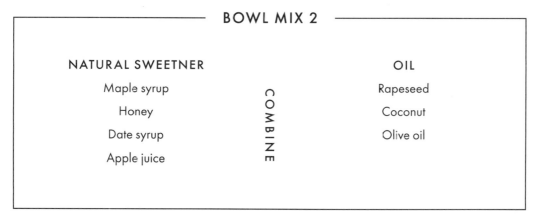

BOWL MIX 2

NATURAL SWEETNER		OIL
Maple syrup		Rapeseed
Honey	COMBINE	Coconut
Date syrup		Olive oil
Apple juice		

BAKE AT 180°C (350°F/GAS 4) IN THE OVEN FOR 30–45 MINUTES

(Remember to turn every 15 minutes)

GRANOLA

___

'Granola is to the world of mainstream breakfast cereals what folk music is to throwaway pop.'

Seb Emina, *The Breakfast Bible* (Bloomsbury Publishing, 2013)

Granola is a baked cereal and is surprisingly simple and easy to make. There are two main components to a granola: your dry and wet ingredients, which can be altered to achieve the flavours and textures you prefer.

You'll find quality granola sits proudly on the shelves of farm shops and delis alike. It's now beginning to make waves on the supermarket aisles, but making it yourself at home means you can enjoy yours warm, straight from the oven. It doesn't have to be for breakfast either – we love a sweet granola just as much, as part of a dessert.

This recipe is inspired by the very first granola that we sold at a market – it has been slowly and steadily tweaked as we received feedback from our customers. We originally included hazelnuts in the recipe, which are still one of our favourite nuts for a granola (and you can easily substitute if you prefer), but eventually settled on the more luxurious pecans. This recipe has stood the test of time and so when we came to choose which granola to start selling in shops in 2015, this was the obvious choice. Annie + Jonny

CINNAMON + PECAN GRANOLA

---

1. Preheat the oven to 180°C (350°F/Gas 4).
2. Combine the dry ingredients in a large bowl.
3. Put all of the wet ingredients into a separate bowl and use a fork or whisk to combine the maple syrup and honey with the oil until emulsified (the colour becomes lighter when this happens). 4. Add the wet ingredients to the dry and mix to ensure that all the oats are covered.
5. Spoon the mixture onto a baking tray lined with baking parchment, spreading it out into a thin, even layer. (Use 2 trays if needed.) 6. Bake on the middle shelf in the oven. After 15 minutes or so, remove the tray from the oven and stir the ingredients thoroughly, spreading them evenly across the tray to prevent the granola from burning at the edges. Return the tray to the oven. The granola is ready when lightly browned (normally 30–35 minutes) and will crisp up as it cools.

Makes around 10 bowls

Dry ingredients
235 g (8 oz/2 cups) oats (oatmeal)
75 g (2½ oz/⅓ cups) coconut flakes
40 g (1½ oz/⅓ cup) pecan nuts
½ teaspoon ground cinnamon
pinch of salt

Wet ingredients
1½ tablespoons maple syrup
60 ml (2 fl oz/¼ cup) honey
50 ml (1½ fl oz/scant ¼ cup) rapeseed oil
1 teaspoon vanilla extract

LIGHT LENTIL GRANOLA

1. Preheat the oven to 180°C (350°F/Gas 4).
2. First, cook the lentils in a pan of boiling water for about 15 minutes, until 'al dente'. Drain, then leave them to cool and pat dry. 3. To 'puff' the amaranth, place a heavy-based pan over a medium heat and let it get hot. Test the heat by adding one or two of the amaranth grains to the pan. They should pop (like popcorn) pretty much straight away. Add 1 tablespoon at a time and put the lid on the pan, moving the pan constantly. The whole batch should be puffed in 20–30 seconds. Once done, set aside in a bowl to cool and make the next batch. 4. Setting the cranberries aside, combine all of the dry ingredients in a large bowl. 5. Put all of the wet ingredients into a separate bowl and use a fork or whisk to emulsify the maple syrup with the oil (the colour becomes lighter when this happens). 6. Add the wet ingredients to the dry and mix to ensure that all the ingredients are well combined.
7. Spoon the mixture onto a baking tray lined with baking parchment and spread it into a thin, even layer. (Use 2 trays if needed.) 8. Place the tray on the middle shelf in the oven and bake for 18–20 minutes. Remove the tray after 10 minutes and stir the ingredients thoroughly, spreading them evenly across the tray to prevent the granola from burning at the edges. The granola will crisp up as it cools and have a really crunchy texture (much more so than with oat-based granola). 9. Add the cranberries to the cooled granola.

Makes around 8 bowls

Dry ingredients
175 g (6 oz/¾ cup) red lentils
4 tablespoons amaranth
60 g (2 oz/⅓ cup) quinoa flakes
60 g (2 oz/1 cup) coconut flakes
4 tablespoons puffed rice
60 g (2 oz/½ cup) dried cranberries

Wet ingredients
200 ml (7 fl oz/scant ⅔ cup)
   maple syrup
2 tablespoons rapeseed oil
1 tablespoon vanilla extract
½ teaspoon ground cardamom
½ teaspoon salt
zest of 1 medium orange

This granola has been a real revelation. The flavours come from the first granola we sold at a Christmas market, using orange zest and cranberries. It was an instant classic and we always sold out. It is amazingly crunchy and incredibly light and you would never guess that lentils are one of the chief components. As all of the ingredients are cooked beforehand, this granola needs less time in the oven than some of the others and crisps up really well as it cools.

Amaranth isn't technically a grain like oats or rice. It's sometimes called a 'pseudo-cereal' – great for those with gluten intolerances – and can be bought in most health food shops. Jonny

BLACK FOREST GRANOLA
WITH CHERRY YOGHURT
+ CHERRY COMPOTE

————

1. Preheat the oven to 180°C (350°F/Gas 4).
2. Combine the dry ingredients in a large bowl. 3. Put all of the wet ingredients into a separate bowl and use a fork or whisk to emulsify the maple syrup and honey with the oil (the colour becomes lighter when this happens). 4. Add the wet mixture to the dry and stir to combine, ensuring that all the oats are covered. 5. Spoon the mixture onto a baking tray lined with baking parchment and spread it into a thin, even layer. (Use 2 trays if needed.) 6. Bake on the middle shelf in the oven. After 15 minutes or so, remove the tray from the oven and stir the ingredients thoroughly, spreading them evenly across the tray to prevent the granola from burning at the edges. Return to the oven. The granola is ready when lightly browned (normally 30–40 minutes) and will crisp up as it cools. 7. To make the cherry yoghurt, remove the stones from the cherries and blend with the yoghurt until smooth. 8. To make the cherry compote, remove the stones from the cherries. Place the cherries in a saucepan with the water. Cover and cook gently over a medium heat until the cherries are soft (around 15 minutes). For a slightly thicker consistency, take the lid off the pan for the last few minutes of cooking.
9. Serve the granola with the yoghurt and compote spooned over.

Makes around 10 generous bowls

Dry ingredients
350 g (12 oz/2¾ cups) jumbo oats
100 g (3½ oz /¾ cup) hazelnuts
   (I like to use them whole)
100 g (3½ oz/⅔ cup) dried cherries
2 heaped tablespoons cocoa powder

Wet ingredients
200 g (7 oz/⅔ cup) honey or maple
   syrup
4 tablespoons rapeseed oil
1 tablespoon vanilla extract

Cherry yoghurt
(per person)
around 5 cherries
75 ml (2 ½ fl oz/¼ cup) good-
   quality Greek yoghurt

Cherry compote
(per person)
around 5 cherries
60 ml (2 fl oz/¼ cup) water

Sometimes you need something slightly more decadent
for your start to the day, and this is the granola I turn
to when that is the case. The combination of chocolate and
cherries is hard to beat. This is just as good as a dessert.
Jonny

LEMON + CARAWAY GRANOLA WITH PEACH COMPOTE

––––––

The name of this granola recipe has changed a few times as we have refined it. The lemon creates a fresh citrus taste, but it's the caraway seeds that really give it a massive flavour boost. For me, caraway seeds are such a Scandinavian taste – it must be something to do with the rye bread I had when I visited.

In any case, this is one of my favourite granola recipes and it is a really grown-up one. Give it to those of your friends who scoff at the lack of sophistication in breakfast foods and see what they think! It's delicious served with some yoghurt. Jonny

1. Preheat the oven to 180°C (350°F/Gas 4).
2. Combine the dry ingredients (except the dried apricots) in a large bowl. 3. Melt the coconut oil gently in a small pan over a medium heat. Pour into a separate bowl, add the remaining wet ingredients, and use a fork or whisk to emulsify the maple syrup and honey with the oil (the colour becomes lighter when this happens). 4. Add the wet ingredients to the dry and mix to ensure that all the oats are covered. 5. Spoon the mixture onto a baking tray lined with baking parchment, spreading it into a thin, even layer. (Use 2 trays if needed.) 6. Bake on the middle shelf in the oven. After 15 minutes or so, remove the tray from the oven and stir the ingredients thoroughly, spreading them evenly across the tray to prevent the granola from burning at the edges. Return to the oven. The granola is ready when lightly browned (normally 30–35 minutes) and will crisp up as it cools. 7. Remove from the oven and leave to cool. Stir in the apricots. 8. To make the peach compote, remove the stones from the peaches, slice the flesh and cut it into small pieces. Put the peaches in a pan along with the remaing compote ingredients. Warm over a medium heat, cover the pan and cook until the peaches are soft – around 20 minutes. 9. Serve the granola with the peach compote and some yoghurt.

Makes 8–10 bowls

Dry ingredients

125 g (4 oz/1 cup) oats (oatmeal)
100 g (3½ oz/⅔ cup) blanched almonds
75 g (2½ oz/½ cup) pumpkin seeds
1 tablespoon sesame seeds
2 teaspoons caraway seeds
1 teaspoon fennel seeds
½ teaspoon ground cinnamon
100 g (3½ oz/½ cup) dried apricots

Wet ingredients

3 tablespoons coconut oil
125 ml (4 fl oz/⅓ cup) maple syrup
3 tablespoons rapeseed oil
zest and juice of 1 lemon

Peach compote

5 ripe peaches
2 tablespoons maple syrup
zest and juice of 1 lemon
2 tablespoons water
zest and juice of 1 lemon

Topping

natural yoghurt

Honey is a go-to ingredient for many granola recipes. It takes centre stage on our breakfast tables and can be infused with all kinds of flavours.

The subtle hint of thyme provides another layer of interest to what would otherwise be just another honey granola. For a slightly lighter granola, you can replace the olive oil with rapeseed oil. Annie

HONEY + THYME GRANOLA
WITH NATURAL YOGHURT + BLOOD ORANGE

————

1. Preheat the oven to 180°C (350°F/Gas 4).
2. Place the honey and half of the thyme sprigs in a pan. Bring to a medium heat and allow the thyme to infuse for up to 10 minutes. 3. Strip the leaves from the remaining thyme sprigs, finely chop (you need about 1 teaspoon's worth) and add to a large mixing bowl with the oats, rye flakes, pine nuts and salt. 4. Take the honey off the heat and carefully remove the sprigs of thyme with a slotted spoon. Add the olive oil and orange zest to the pan and mix well. 5. Pour the honey mixture into the dry ingredients and stir well to combine. 6. Spoon the mixture onto a baking tray lined with baking parchment, spreading it into a thin, even layer. (Use 2 trays if needed.) 7. Bake in the oven for 30–45 minutes, removing the tray every 15 minutes to stir the ingredients, spreading them evenly across the tray to prevent the granola from burning at the edges. Return the tray to the oven. The granola is ready when lightly browned and will crisp up as it cools. 8. Take the granola out of the oven and to leave to cool. 9. Serve with the segments of blood orange and yoghurt.

Makes 8–10 bowls

125 ml (4 fl oz/⅓ cup) honey
20 g (¾ oz/small bunch) fresh thyme
125 g (4 oz/1 cup) jumbo oats
125 g (4 oz/1 cup) rye flakes
40 g (1½ oz/¼ cup) pine nuts
pinch of salt
100 ml (3½ fl oz/¼ cup) olive oil
zest of ½ orange

Topping
sliced segments of blood oranges
natural yoghurt

You could describe this granola as a 'healthy Bombay mix', which adds a little spicy kick to the cooling and creamy avocado. I love this when I'm craving something savoury in the morning or for a light lunch. This recipe makes a big batch, which can be enjoyed throughout the week. Annie

AVOCADO WITH SAVOURY GRANOLA CRUNCH

1. Preheat the oven to 180°C (350°F/Gas 4). 2. Place all the dry ingredients in a large mixing bowl and mix to ensure everything is evenly combined. 3. Melt the coconut oil in a small pan over a medium heat. Pour it into the dry ingredients and stir to combine. 4. Spoon the mixture onto a baking tray lined with baking parchment, spreading it into a thin, even layer. (Use 2 trays if needed.) 5. Bake on the middle shelf in the oven for 15 minutes, removing the tray from the oven and stirring the ingredients thoroughly halfway through, spreading them evenly across the tray to prevent the granola from burning at the edge. Bake until the mixture starts to colour, then remove from the oven and leave to cool. 6. Garnish with a handful of raisins or sultanas to add a little sweet hit, if you like. 7. Slice the avocado in half and remove the stone. Place in a bowl and sprinkle your savoury granola on top.

Makes 8 bowls

handful of raisins or sultanas (optional), to garnish
1 avocado, to serve

Dry ingredients
125 g (4 oz/1 cup) spelt
125 g (4 oz/1 cup) oats (oatmeal)
2 tablespoons pumpkin seeds
60 g (2 oz/⅓ cup) cashew nuts, roughly chopped
1 teaspoon turmeric
1 teaspoon ground cinnamon
½ teaspoon ground ginger
pinch of salt
½ teaspoon dried chilli flakes

Wet ingredients
60 ml (2 fl oz/¼ cup) coconut oil

Bananas are a breakfast staple for me and I probably include them in my breakfast on most days. We have tried several variants of a banana granola in the Spoon Cereals kitchen over the years but this recipe has come out the winner, as bananas and walnuts are such a great combination. Simplicity, great taste and solid nutritional benefits mean that this granola epitomises what our cereals are all about. Jonny

BANANA + WALNUT GRANOLA

---

1. Preheat the oven to 200°C (375°F/Gas 6).
2. Combine the dry ingredients (except the dried banana chips) in a large mixing bowl. 3. Mash the bananas until soft and smooth. Put all of the wet ingredients into a separate bowl and mix thoroughly. 4. Add the wet ingredients to the dry and mix to ensure everything is well combined. 5. Spoon the mixture onto a baking tray lined with baking parchment, spreading into a thin, even layer. (Use 2 trays if needed.) 6. Bake on the middle shelf in the oven, turning the ingredients every 15 minutes or so and spreading them evenly across the tray, to prevent the granola from burning at the edges. The granola is ready when lightly browned (normally 30–35 minutes) and should crisp up as it cools. If the granola is not yet crisp (the bananas do add a bit of extra moisture) you can turn off the oven and leave it in there while it cools down.
7. Remove the granola from the oven. Break up the dry banana chips to the size you want and then add them to the granola.

Makes 8–10 bowls

Dry ingredients
175 g (6 oz/1 ⅓ cups) oats (oatmeal)
75 g (2 ½ oz/¾ cup) walnut halves
1 teaspoon ground cinnamon
60 g (2 oz/½ cup) dried banana chips

Wet ingredients
2 ripe bananas, peeled
125 ml (4 fl oz/⅓ cup) maple syrup
100 ml (3 ½ fl oz/⅓ cup) rapeseed oil

I was inspired to create this recipe after making the chocolate and lime mud cake from one of my favourite baking books, *Crumb* by Ruby Tandoh (Chatto & Windus Ltd, 2014). I'd always recommend using good-quality dark chocolate (between 70–80 per cent cocoa solids).

For a lighter granola, leave out the extra dark chocolate; but I'm not sure Ruby would approve of this, so I like to keep it in! Annie

CHOCOLATE + LIME GRANOLA

1. Preheat the oven to 180°C (350°F/Gas 4).
2. Combine all the dry ingredients together in a mixing bowl. 3. Melt the coconut oil gently in a pan over a medium heat. Stir in the maple syrup and lime juice until combined. 4. Pour the oil and syrup mixture into the dry ingredients and mix together. 5. Spoon the mixture onto a baking tray lined with baking parchment, spreading it into a thin, even layer. (Use 2 trays if needed.) 6. Bake on the middle shelf in the oven for 15 minutes. Remove from the oven, scatter the dark chocolate over the granola and return to the oven to cook for a further 10–15 minutes until the chocolate has melted. 7. Remove from the oven and ensure the oats are evenly coated with the melted chocolate by stirring with a wooden spoon. 8. Grate the lime zest straight on top of the granola and stir into the mix. Leave to cool. 9. Make your yoghurt by blending the lime yoghurt with the lime zest and juice. Serve in bowls, topped with the granola.

Makes 8–10 bowls

60 g (2 oz) dark chocolate (at least
   70% cocoa solids), finely chopped
zest of 1 lime

Dry ingredients
250 g (9 oz/2 cups) oats (oatmeal)
60 g (2 oz/⅓ cup) whole blanched
   almonds, roughly chopped
1 heaped tablespoon cocoa powder
pinch of salt

Wet ingredients
60 ml (2 fl oz/¼ cup) coconut oil
60 ml (2 fl oz/¼ cup) maple syrup
juice of 1 lime

Lime yoghurt (serves 2)
200 ml (7 fl oz/¾ cup) natural
   yoghurt
juice and zest of 1 lime

I befriended food photograper Hugh Johnson in my advertising days, when we worked together on numerous food photography shoots. Not only has he been incredibly supportive, he has also been responsible for all our product photography and loaned us his studio for events.

Life's too short not to enjoy pudding for breakfast once in a while. However, if it's a healthier version you're after, Hugh recommends using Greek yoghurt instead of mascarpone and sugar. Annie

BREAKFAST TIRAMISU

1. Put the mascarpone or yoghurt into a large bowl, add the vanilla extract and, if using mascarpone, the sugar. Mix until smooth using a wooden spoon. 2. Divide half the granola among individual glasses. Pour in the skimmed milk. Top with half the berries and half the mascarpone (or yoghurt) mixture. 3. Repeat the layers, finishing off with the mascarpone (or yoghurt) mixture. 4. Before serving, scatter with extra granola to add a nice crunch.

Makes 4–6 individual glasses

255 g (9 oz/1 ¼ cups) mascarpone cheese or Greek yoghurt

1 teaspoon vanilla extract

1 tablespoon caster (superfine) sugar (if using mascarpone)

150 g (5 oz/1 cup) Cinnamon + Pecan Granola (page 25), or another favourite granola, plus extra to garnish

100 ml (3 ½ fl oz/⅓ cup) skimmed milk

500 g (1 lb 2 oz/3 ½ cups) mixed fresh summer berries and fruits (such as strawberries, blueberries, raspberries and cherries)

This is our version of the ice cream sandwich – an up-to-date version of a childhood favourite, which makes a great dessert or treat for a summer brunch. It's very simple: the ice cream is actually just made of fruit. Banana ice cream is a real favourite and, though this one includes mango for a tropical twist, it can easily be adapted using other fruits and flavours. I normally use a ratio of 2:1 bananas to mango to make a nice smooth blend. Try adding some cocoa powder for a chocolate version or a few summer fruits for a red berry ice cream. Jonny

GRANOLA ICE CREAM SANDWICH

———

1. Preheat the oven to 200°C (375°F/Gas 6).
2. To make the cookies, combine all the ingredients in a large bowl and mix well. 3. Lightly grease a baking tray. Divide the mixture into 8 portions and place them on the tray, spacing them well apart. Flatten them gently with your hands. 4. Bake in the oven for 15–18 minutes, until the cookies are just turning brown. Remove and allow to cool. 5. For the ice cream, slice the bananas and mango into small pieces. Put in the freezer for at least 3 hours.
6. Once the fruit is frozen, put it in a smoothie maker or food processor and blend until smooth. 7. To serve, spoon the banana ice cream mix between two cookies and enjoy!

Serves 4

Cookies
60 g (2 oz/½ cup) jumbo oats
60 g (2 oz/½ cup) quinoa flakes
2 tablespoons desiccated coconut
75 g (2½ oz/1⅓ cup) maple syrup
125 g (4 oz/½ cup) smooth nut
    butter (such as peanut)
zest and juice of 1 lime
butter, for greasing

Ice cream
2 bananas, peeled
1 ripe mango, peeled (or frozen
    mango pieces to the same
    quantity)

MUESLI

Muesli is basically the lighter version of granola, and sometimes gets a bit of a bad rap for being bland and boring. Grains, nuts, seeds and dried fruit form the basis, and we can promise you the recipes that follow are anything but dull.

We love cooking up batches of granola and mixing mueslis in our kitchens, and there have been some shockers when experiments haven't always gone to plan. From the hundreds of batches made, we've learned from our mistakes and stumbled across new tricks. Incorporating spices and lightly toasting the grains makes for a more exciting and flavourful recipe without the need for added sugars or oils.

We recommend making large batches at home and storing in an airtight or clip top jar. This way you can enjoy muesli bowls with your preferred nuts and fruits throughout the week. These are best enjoyed with milk or yoghurt and seasonal fresh fruit or compotes.

To create a nutty, wholesome-tasting muesli, the trick is to toast your grains and nuts. This also gives your bowl a lovely crispy texture. Ground ginger is a fantastic ingredient to use. It keeps the sugar content down and its warm, zesty and spicy aromas, together with fresh lemon juice, create a light, uplifting breakfast. Annie

TOASTED LEMON + GINGER MUESLI

1. Preheat the oven to 180°C (350°F/Gas 4). 2. Soak the almonds in the lemon juice for 20 minutes. Drain the almonds. 3. Put all the dry ingredients, except for the dried apricots, into a mixing bowl, add the soaked almonds and stir to combine. 4. Melt the coconut oil in a small pan over a medium heat. 5. Pour the coconut oil over the dry ingredients and mix well. 6. Line a baking tray with baking parchment and spoon the mixture on top, spreading it across the tray to form an even layer. (Use 2 trays if necessary.) 7. Bake in the oven on the middle shelf for 15–20 minutes, turning after 5 minutes. 8. Remove from the oven and add the lemon zest, stirring to combine. Garnish with dried apricots. Leave to cool.

Makes 8–10 bowls

150 g (5 oz/1 cup) blanched
    almonds, roughly chopped
juice of 2 lemons
60 ml (2 fl oz/¼ cup) coconut oil
zest of 1 lemon, to garnish

Dry ingredients
250 g (9 oz/2 cups) oats (oatmeal)
30 g (1 oz/1 cup) puffed rice
2 teaspoons ground ginger
2 teaspoons ground cinnamon
30 g (1 oz/½ cup) coconut flakes
pinch of salt
60 g (2 oz/⅓ cup) dried apricots,
    roughly chopped

Makes 8–10 bowls

200 g (7 oz/2 cups) Cinnamon
 + Pecan Granola (page 25)
100 g (3½ oz/¾ cup) jumbo oats
100 g (3½ oz/¾ cup) rye flakes
20 g (¾ oz/⅔ cup) puffed rice
2 tablespoons chopped Brazil nuts
2 tablespoons pumpkin seeds
1 tablespoon freeze-dried berries

Toppings
milk (any kind)
pomegranate seeds
freeze-dried berries

1. Combine all the ingredients in a large mixing bowl. 2. Enjoy with a cold splash of milk, a sprinkling of pomegranate seeds and more freeze-dried berries for an extra berry kick.

MUESLI + GRANOLA MIX

I love the slow-release energy a large bowl of muesli provides. This muesli, combined with a sprinkling of granola, adds the perfect amount of sweetness and is one of my fail-safe morning rituals.

The muesli in this recipe includes puffed rice as well as freeze-dried berries. These create a tangy burst of flavour that seeps into your milk if you give it enough time! The recipe incorporates our award-winning Cinnamon + Pecan Granola (page 25) – giving you the best of both worlds. Annie

Muesli is something that I grew up eating. It was the shop-bought, highly sugared stuff that I could not get enough of when I was young. Now, as an adult, I find that muesli still has associations with time spent in Germany and Switzerland, where it originates, and where I have spent quite a bit of time working. I have always enjoyed mueslis that are on the lighter side and this one fits the bill perfectly. It is also a gluten-free recipe, which is something that we have been asked about innumerable times at our market stall and food fairs. Gluten-free mueslis can be dry and 'dusty', due to the small size of the flakes – something we have tried to avoid here. In simple recipes such as this one and Mountain Muesli (page 54), the easiest thing to do is to work with ratios of ingredients – this way, you can make as little or as much as you want. I find it best just to use a cup as a unit of measurement, which also makes it much easier to tweak the recipe to your taste. So, for example, if you use half a cup of oats in the recipe below, it will make around 500 g (17½ oz/4½ cups) muesli in total. Jonny

SUMMER MUESLI

1. Combine all the ingredients in a bowl and enjoy with your favourite milk. 1. This tastes great with a nut milk (of your choice) and some fresh summer fruits.

Makes 8–10 bowls

170 g (6 oz/1 cup) buckwheat flakes
95 g (3½ oz/½ cup) dried apricots
65 g (2¼ oz/½ cup) Brazil nut pieces
65 g (2¼ oz/½ cup) pumpkin seeds
50 g (2 oz/½ cup) cup oats (oatmeal)
50 g (2 oz/½ cup) dried mango, cut
   into small pieces
25 g (¾ oz/1 cup) puffed rice

Toppings
nut milk (any kind)
fresh summer fruits, to serve

A breakfast bowl is just as much about the texture as it is about the flavour. When I'm not after a smooth and creamy porridge on a winter's morning, I often crave a bit of crunch.

I like to be taken out of my morning bowl comfort zone once in while by replacing the humble oat in a classic bowl of muesli with ingredients like buckwheat, coconut chips and cashew nuts. In this recipe, these ingredients are toasted with a little coconut oil. Annie

TOASTED BUCKWHEAT
WITH CRANBERRIES + FREEZE-DRIED BERRIES

1. Preheat the oven to 180°C (350°F/Gas 4).
2. Mix all the dry ingredients, except for the dried cranberries, in a large mixing bowl.
3. Melt the coconut oil in a small pan over a medium heat. 4. Pour the oil over the dry ingredients and stir to combine. 5. Spoon the mixture onto a baking tray lined with baking parchment, spreading it out and patting it down with a wooden spoon. (Use 2 trays if necessary.)
6. Place on the middle shelf in the oven. Bake for 15 minutes, turning the mixture after 5 minutes. 7. Remove from the oven, add the dried cranberries and leave to cool. 8. Serve with your favourite milk or yoghurt and the suggested fruit toppings.

Makes 8–10 bowls

3 tablespoons coconut oil, melted

Dry ingredients
375 g (13 oz/2 cups) buckwheat groats
1 tablespoon coconut flakes
2 tablespoons flaked almonds
2 tablespoons chopped cashew nuts
2 tablespoons sunflower seeds
45 g (1½ oz/¼ cup) dried cranberries

Toppings
milk or yoghurt (any kind)
freeze-dried berries
blueberries
pomegranate seeds

I was introduced to Anna Pinder, trained chef and food consultant, by a mutual friend, and we bonded over our obsession with good-quality breakfast cereal. *'Cereal has always been a love of mine,'* she says. *'Breakfast, lunch or dinner, I can eat it all day.'* Annie

HOMEMADE BRAN FLAKES

——————

1. Preheat the oven to 160°C (320°F/Gas 3) 2. Place the dry ingredients in a bowl, add the honey and then slowly add the water and milk, mixing well to create a wet dough.
3. Cut 2 sheets of baking parchment to fit 2 baking trays. This is important, to ensure the wet dough doesn't stick.
4. Divide the dough in half and place on the lined trays, flattening it down slightly. Place a piece of cling film (plastic wrap) over the top of the dough and use a rolling pin to roll it evenly flat. It should be spread so thin that it is almost transparent (this way you'll end up with crispy flakes). 5. Remove the cling film (plastic wrap) and place the baking trays in the oven. Cook for 10 minutes, checking after 5 to make sure the dough doesn't burn. Remove from the oven and leave to cool before tearing into flake-sized pieces. 6. Reduce the oven temperature to 110°C (45°F/Gas ¼) and line the trays with fresh baking parchment. Spread the bran flakes on the trays and return to the oven. 7. Cook for a further 15–20 minutes, turning every 5 minutes or so to make sure they cook evenly. 8. Let the bran flakes cool and crisp up before eating. Top with the granola and enjoy with a splash of fresh milk and your berry of choice.

Makes 2 bowls

Dry ingredients
40 g (1½ oz/⅓ cup) ground almonds
60 g (2 oz/⅓ cup) wholewheat flour
60g (2 oz/¾ cup) bran
pinch of sea salt
¼ teaspoon baking powder

Wet ingredients
2 tablespoons honey
60 ml (2 fl oz/¼ cup) water
75 ml (2½ fl oz/⅓ cup) almond milk

Toppings
Cinnamon + Pecan Granola (page 25) or another favourite granola
milk (any kind)
berries (such as blueberries raspberries, strawberries and dried cranberries)

MOUNTAIN MUESLI

——————

This muesli is a classic, and is great for one of those days when you really need something substantial to get through to lunch. It has fuelled the Spoon Cereals team on numerous family skiing holidays and is inspired by the intrepid guide who has led Annie's family up into the mountains many times since they were young. He loves his huge breakfasts! Whichever way you choose to eat it, make sure to bring a big appetite with you. Jonny

Makes 8–10 bowls

250 g (9 oz/2½ cups) jumbo oats
85 g (3 oz/½ cup) buckwheat flakes
65 g (2 oz/½ cup) Brazil nuts,
    roughly chopped
50 g (1½ oz/½ cup) rye flakes
50 g (1½ oz/½ cup) almonds, toasted
35 g (1 oz/¼ cup) sultanas
35 g (1 oz/¼ cup) dried figs
35 g (1 oz/¼ cup) pumpkin seeds
35 g (1 oz/¼ cup) sunflower seeds
35 g (1 oz/¼ cup) linseed (brown
    or golden)
25 g (½ oz/¼ cup) dried bananas chips

Topping
milk or yoghurt (any kind)
banana or red fruit compote (such as
    the berry compote on page 60)

1. Combine all the ingredients in a large mixing bowl. 2. Serve with milk or yoghurt, and either banana or a red fruit compote.

THREE-GRAIN MUESLI

———

I'm often overwhelmed by all the latest food trends that are infiltrating our healthy cereals these days. There is a dizzying array of 'super foods' out there and just as many weird and wacky sugar alternatives.

This recipe, by contrast, is never going to win a prize for innovation, but with its wholesome, simple and infinitely adaptable mix of grains, nuts, seeds and dried fruit, it's a doddle to make, so that I can focus on the more pressing decisions that lie ahead for me each day. Annie

Makes 8–10 bowls

100 g (3½ oz/¾ cup) rye flakes
100 g (3½ oz/¾ cup) jumbo oats
100 g (3½ oz/¾ cup) spelt flakes
60 g (2 oz/⅓ cup) dates, chopped
60 g (2 oz/⅓ cup) dried apricots,
    chopped
2 tablespoons roughly chopped
    hazelnuts
2 tablespoons roughly chopped
    Brazil nuts
2 tablespoons roughly chopped
    almonds
1 tablespoon sunflower seeds

Topping
milk (any kind)
blueberries

1. Combine all the ingredients in a large mixing bowl. 2. Serve with milk and blueberries.

PORRIDGE

We aspire to live simply at Spoon Cereals. It's a way of life that is epitomised by the Nordic regions, making the most of their resources and highlighting the natural qualities of products. In cooking, this simplicity means that even a morning bowl of porridge is something to be treasured, something that feels exciting to eat at all times of the day. We take inspiration from this philosophy when creating our porridge bowls.

At its best, a warming bowl of porridge is the driving force to keep you going through the long winter months. The versatility of porridge means that there is always a version that will satisfy even the strictest dietary requirements and taste buds. What was once seen as something old-fashioned and uninspiring is now turning up very regularly, not only in our breakfast bowls but also in our Instagram feeds and morning conversations.

Throughout the winter months, a warming bowl of porridge is a big part of my weekly breakfast menu. In its simplest form – oats, water and milk – it's the perfect base for all kinds of flavours, meaning you can have a different bowl every day of the week.

Jumbo oats lend themselves perfectly to full-fat (whole) milk; you get a creaminess that just cannot be achieved from other milks. When I'm in need of that extra little boost in the morning, porridge made with a home-brewed cup of coffee and a drizzle of maple syrup is the ultimate pick-me-up. To save time, make batches of toasted walnuts and store for when required. Annie

COFFEE, MAPLE + WALNUT PORRIDGE

————

1. Preheat the oven to 180°C (350°F/Gas 4).
2. Place the walnuts on a baking tray and toast in the oven for 15 minutes, turning after 5 minutes. 3. Meanwhile, put the oats, milk and brewed coffee in a pan and cook over a medium heat for 5–10 minutes. 4. Remove the walnuts from the oven and leave to cool. 5. Spoon the oat mixture into bowls, top with the toasted walnuts and drizzle with maple syrup.

Makes 2–3 bowls

2 tablespoons chopped toasted
   walnuts
125 g (4 oz/1 cup) jumbo oats
250 ml (8½ fl oz/1 cup) full-fat
   (whole) milk
250 ml (8½ fl oz/1 cup)
   home-brewed coffee

Topping
drizzle of maple syrup

With my love for breakfast and minimalistic design, it was only a matter of time before I stumbled across London-based Danish restaurant, Snaps + Rye. The restaurant's understated interior and traditional ingredients transport me to Scandinavia every time I visit. This recipe comes from co-owner, Jacqueline Skott. Annie

'If it's a lazy one, then it has to be eggs Benedict and a glass of bubbles!'
Jacqueline Skott, co-owner of Snaps + Rye

BUTTERMILK PORRIDGE

———

1. Heat a dry frying pan (skillet). Add the nuts and seeds and toast until light brown, tossing frequently to stop them from burning. 2. Preheat the oven to 180°C (350°F/Gas 4). Blitz the rye bread in a food processor and spread the crumbs onto a baking tray. Dot with butter and brown sugar and bake for about 5 minutes. 3. To make the berry compote, put the berries and sugar in a saucepan over a low heat and slowly reduce to a syrup, keeping the berries intact as much as possible. 4. Place all the porridge ingredients in another saucepan and cook gently over a very low heat for about 5 minutes. 5. Taste for sweetness and stir through the toasted rye crumbs, reserving some for sprinkling. Top with the berry compote, toasted nuts and seeds and the remaining rye crumbs.

Makes 2 bowls

60 g (2 oz/½ cup) mixed nuts and seeds
2 thin slices good rye bread
few dots of butter
2 teaspoons soft brown sugar

Berry compote
100 g (3 ½ oz/½ cup) mixed autumn berries (frozen is fine)
2 teaspoons caster (superfine) sugar

Porridge
80 g (3 oz/⅔ cup) jumbo oats
200 ml (7 fl oz/¾ cup) water
200 ml (7 fl oz/¾ cup) buttermilk
4 teaspoons caster (superfine) sugar
pinch of salt

I like to use a variety of different grains in my porridge for a slightly different texture. Rye is a robust grain, giving more of a bite to your bowl. A little extra cooking time is required to achieve a smooth consistency. Annie

RYE + OAT PORRIDGE
WITH KIWI + BANANA CHIPS

—

Makes 2–3 bowls

Porridge
60 g (2 oz/½ cup) rye flakes
60 g (2 oz/½ cup) jumbo oats
250 ml (8 ½ fl oz/1 cup)
   coconut milk
250 ml (8 ½ fl oz/1 cup) water

Toppings
slices of kiwi fruit
dried banana chips

1. Place all the ingredients for the porridge in a saucepan and cook over a medium heat for 5–10 minutes. 2. Spoon the mixture into bowls and serve topped with sliced kiwi fruit and banana chips. Fresh banana will also work nicely.

Makes 2–3 bowls

200 g (7 oz/1 cup) millet flakes
250 ml (8½ fl oz/1 cup) milk (any
 kind)
250 ml (8½ fl oz/1 cup) water

Toppings
Maple Butter (page 119)
diced pear
pumpkin seeds

1. Place all the ingredients for the porridge in a pan and cook over a medium heat for 5–10 minutes. 2. Spoon into bowls and serve topped with a drizzle of Maple Butter, diced pear and a sprinkling of pumpkin seeds.

MILLET PORRIDGE
WITH FRESH PEAR + MAPLE BUTTER

Millet flakes make a lovely, smooth porridge. But the real game changer in this bowl is Jonny's Maple Butter (page 119) drizzled on top and finished with a handful of freshly chopped pear and pumpkin seeds. Annie

This compote was developed on a cold winter's day. It was inspired by my dad and his love of marmalade on toast in the mornings, which, to me, epitomises the breakfasts of my childhood. It has proved a popular choice at our pop-up breakfast bar.

I'll often serve this on top of porridge with a sprinkling of our Cinnamon + Pecan Granola (page 25) for an added crispy texture. Annie

OAT PORRIDGE
WITH ORANGE, MARMALADE + THYME COMPOTE

1. To make the compote, peel the oranges and discard any pith. 2. Using a sharp knife, segment the oranges to get the juiciest part of the fruit, collecting any juices. 3. Bring the orange flesh and juices to the boil in a pan with the thyme and marmalade. Leave to simmer gently for about 30 minutes, then remove from the heat and leave to cool. 4. To make the porridge, place all the ingredients in a pan and cook over a medium heat for 5–10 minutes. 5. Divide the porridge into bowls. Top with a spoonful of the compote and a scattering of the granola.

Makes 2–3 bowls

Orange, marmalade + thyme compote
6 oranges
5 fresh thyme sprigs
1 tablespoon marmalade

Porridge
125 g (4 oz/1 cup) oats (oatmeal)
250 ml (8½ fl oz/1 cup) water
250 ml (8½ fl oz/1 cup) milk
  (any kind)

Topping
Cinnamon + Pecan Granola
  (page 25)

Often confined to toast in the mornings, avocado on porridge may sound odd but the squeeze of lemon lifts the taste and when topped with the sweet chilli, provides a perfect harmony of flavours. Annie

AVOCADO PORRIDGE WITH SWEET CHILLI

1. To make the sweet chilli jam, deseed the chilli and slice it into thin strips. Place the chilli and honey in a pan over a medium heat and cook for 5 minutes until it forms an almost jam-like consistency. 2. To make the porridge, place all the ingredients in a pan and cook over a medium heat for 5–10 minutes. 3. Slice the avocado in half and remove the skin and stone. Then slice each half into thin strips. 4. Divide the porridge into bowls and top with the avocado and a drizzle of the sweet chilli jam.

Makes 2–3 bowls

Sweet chilli jam
½ fresh red chilli
2 tablespoons honey

Porridge
125 g (4 oz/1 cup) oats (oatmeal)
250 ml (8½ fl oz/1 cup) water
250 ml (8½ fl oz/1 cup) milk
   (any kind)
squeeze of lemon juice

Topping
1 ripe avocado

Banana porridge is one of the simplest recipes there is, but you can transform it into a really indulgent breakfast with a topping of almonds and amaretti. The distinct almond-apricot taste of the amaretti biscuits really complements the banana flavour. We use this topping when we take our pop-up cereal bar out to markets and it's always very popular. And we don't really need an excuse to have some biscuits for breakfast now and then, do we? Jonny

BANANA PORRIDGE WITH ALMONDS + AMARETTI

———

1. Add the oats and milk to a pan, heating through and stirring until the liquid is absorbed and the porridge is smooth and creamy.
2. Mash the bananas and add to the cooked porridge together with the maple syrup or honey, and stir through. 3. Toast the flaked almonds under the grill or in a dry pan until they have a little colour (being careful that they do not burn). Crush the amaretti biscuits. 4. Spoon your cooked porridge into bowls, add an extra splash of milk, if you like, and sprinkle over the toasted almonds and crushed biscuits.

Makes 3–4 bowls

175 g (6 oz/1¼ cups) oats (oatmeal)
550 ml (19 fl oz/2¼ cups) milk (any kind) or water
2 ripe bananas, peeled
2 tablespoons maple syrup or honey
2 tablespoons flaked almonds
2 tablespoons amaretti biscuits
milk of your choice (optional)

'Only after I've had my bowl of grains, fruit, berries and nut milk in various forms and finished a chapter in my book while sipping strong black tea, only then can my day begin.'

Agnes Gällhagen,
food blogger, *Cashew Kitchen*

SAVOURY PORRIDGE

WITH LEMON-ROASTED FENNEL, BEETROOT CHIPS, BASIL OIL + SUNFLOWER 'PARMESAN'

At Spoon Cereals, we have been eating increasingly vegetarian food over the last few years. When we first started eating less meat, being creative with our recipes did not come easily and we needed some serious inspiration. Enter Agnes. She creates amazing vegetarian food and makes it all look effortlessly beautiful. This savoury recipe might look daunting with its various components, but they are all easy to prepare if you have a bit of time. And everything apart from the porridge can be done in advance. Trust me, the effort will certainly be worth it. Annie

Makes 4 bowls

Lemon-roasted fennel
1 large fennel bulb
olive oil
½ lemon
salt and freshly ground black pepper
3 tablespoons water

Beetroot chips
3 beetroots (beets)
drizzle of olive oil
pinch of salt

Basil oil
6 fresh basil sprigs, including stems
5 tablespoons olive oil

Sunflower 'Parmesan'
140 g (4½ oz/1 cup) sunflower
    seeds
2 tablespoons olive oil
4 tablespoons nutritional yeast
    flakes*
1 teaspoon agave syrup
pinch of fine sea salt

Porridge
125 g (4 oz/1 cup) oats (oatmeal),
    rinsed and soaked for at least
    6 hours
olive oil
½ onion, finely chopped
2 garlic cloves, finely chopped
1 celery stalk, finely chopped
750 ml (24 fl oz/3 cups) vegetable
    stock, or 500ml (17 fl oz/2 cups)
    water plus 1 ½ vegetable stock
    cubes
pinch of dried chilli flakes
3–4 thyme sprigs or 1 ½ teaspoons
    dried thyme
125 ml (4 fl oz/½ cup) white wine
juice of ¼ lemon
2 tablespoons oat cream or cream
    of choice
1 tablespoon nutritional yeast flakes
1–2 teaspoons agave syrup
freshly ground black pepper

*   *Nutritional yeast is a vegan, inactive yeast rich in B vitamins.
    It comes in powder or flakes and has a pleasant nutty and cheesy
    flavour. Sprinkle it on pasta or popcorn, or use it in vegan sauces
    or pesto to give a delicious cheesy twist.*

1. Preheat the oven to 200°C (400°F/Gas 6).
2. Quarter the fennel and remove the hard stalks. Rinse thoroughly. Put in an ovenproof dish and drizzle with the olive oil. Zest the lemon, then cut in half and squeeze the juice from one quarter. Add the lemon zest, lemon juice, salt and pepper to the dish. Pour over the water and roast for 35–45 minutes, turning the fennel pieces over halfway through. 3. To make the beetroot chips, heat the oven to 150°C (300°F/Gas 2). Peel and thinly slice the beetroots, using a sharp knife or a mandoline. 4. Spread out the beetroot slices on a baking tray lined with baking parchment. Drizzle with just a little olive oil and sprinkle with salt. Massage the oil into the beetroot slices. Be careful not to add too much oil. Make sure the beetroot slices are spread out evenly (some overlapping is fine) and roast for 1–2 hours (depending on desired crispiness). Turn off the oven and leave to cool inside, where they will crisp up. Store in a paper bag at room temperature. 5. Roughly chop the basil and blend with the olive oil using a handheld blender. Store at room temperature until ready to use. 6. To make the sunflower 'Parmesan', lightly toast the sunflower seeds in a frying pan (skillet) until fragrant and slightly browned. Leave to cool. Finely chop the sunflower seeds, leaving some coarse pieces, and place in a

bowl. Combine with the olive oil, yeast flakes and agave syrup. Season to taste. This keeps well in a jar in the fridge for about 1–2 weeks. 7. For the porridge, soak the oats in plenty of water overnight (or in the morning, if you're planning to make it in the evening). 8. Discard the soaking water and place the oats along with some oil, the onion, garlic and celery in a large pan. Stir-fry over a medium heat until fragrant. 9. Heat the vegetable stock (or water and stock cube) in a separate pan. The stock should be salty but not overly so. 10. Add half of the stock to the oats and leave to simmer over a medium–low heat until the stock is reduced by about half. Then add the chilli and thyme. Keep adding more stock to the oats gradually, increasing the amount as it reduces. Stir occasionally, then more often, as the porridge cooks. 11. Once all the stock is used and the oatmeal starts to develop a risotto-like consistency, add the wine and lemon juice. Leave to simmer, stirring occasionally for a minute or so. Add the oat cream, yeast flakes, agave syrup and pepper, and leave to simmer for a moment until the porridge has reached the consistency you like. Taste and add more pepper, chilli or salt if you like. 12. Serve the porridge topped with the roasted fennel and beetroot chips. Scatter over the sunflower 'Parmesan' and finish with a drizzle of the basil oil.

BIRCHER

——

Also described as 'overnight oats', Bircher muesli requires soaking oats, traditionally in apple juice and yoghurt, for up to four hours.

Bircher does need some advance thought, but making it the night before, ensuring there are a few empty jars knocking about your kitchen in which to store it, makes mornings a lot more straightforward. It's a convenient breakfast that's ready to eat as soon as you get up or can be popped into your bag and enjoyed at work.

I love the freshness and creaminess of oats left to soak overnight with a little bit of citrus and fruit. It is a great start to the day, whatever you have going on later. Blackberries are, for me, a very nostalgic taste – I used to pick them by the basketful as a child, in the bushes behind the house I grew up in, adjacent to the underground tracks. I love that you never know how sharp or sweet the taste will be. They make a classic combination with the fresh taste of apples in this compote, with just a little sweetness added. I return to this Bircher time and time again. Jonny

BLACKBERRY + APPLE BIRCHER

―――――――

1. Put all the ingredients for the Bircher in a bowl and mix thoroughly. 2. Cover and place in the fridge overnight. 3. To make the blackberry compote, put all the ingredients in a pan over a medium heat and cook until the blackberries are soft but have not lost their shape. 4. Serve the compote on top of the Bircher, with fresh slices of apple, if you wish.

Makes 2 bowls

Bircher
100 g (3½ oz/¾ cup) oats (oatmeal)
¼ teaspoon ground cinnamon
1½ red apples, peeled and grated
zest of ½ lemon
250 ml (8½ fl oz/1 cup) of milk (any kind)
½ tablespoon maple syrup or honey

Blackberry compote
175 g (6 oz/¾ cup) blackberries
2 tablespoons water
½ tablespoon maple syrup or honey

Topping
slices of red apple (optional)

I know my body is thanking me when I incorporate vegetables into my breakfast bowl. Grated carrot is a great one to sneak in there, adding flavour, nutrients, texture and colour. When preparing this recipe before bed, I know I have something to look forward to in the morning. Annie

SPICED CARROT BIRCHER

1. Place all the ingredients for the Bircher in a mixing bowl and stir to combine. 2. Cover and place in the fridge overnight. 3. The next morning, divide the mixture between 2 bowls. Serve with the suggested toppings.

Makes 2 bowls

Bircher
100 g (3½ oz/¾ cup) oats (oatmeal)
100 ml (3½ fl oz/⅓ cup) milk (any kind)
100 ml (3½ fl oz/⅓ cup) natural yoghurt
60 ml (2 fl oz/¼ cup) water
1 carrot, peeled and grated
½ apple, peeled and grated
1 teaspoon maple syrup
½ teaspoon ground cinnamon
¼ teaspoon ground nutmeg

Toppings
dried dates
walnuts
maple syrup (for those with a sweet tooth)

Who doesn't love a pistachio nut? Whizzing them to a dust brings out their almost fluorescent colour and it's a topping we've often used to give our breakfast bowls the 'wow factor'. Perfect over a bowl of classic apple Bircher. Annie

GREEN APPLE BIRCHER WITH PISTACHIOS

Makes 2 bowls

Bircher
125 g (4 oz/1 cup) oats (oatmeal)
100 ml (3 ½ fl oz/⅓ cup) almond milk
100 ml (3 ½ fl oz/⅓ cup) apple juice
1 green apple, peeled and grated
zest of 1 lime
1 teaspoon maple syrup

Toppings
blitzed pistachios
slices of green apple

1. Place all the ingredients for the Bircher in a mixing bowl and stir to combine. 2. Cover and place in the fridge overnight. 3. The next morning, divide the mixture between 2 bowls. Serve with the suggested toppings.

Not only does beetroot add vibrancy to your morning Bircher, it also increases levels of antioxidant enzymes in the body. I love its earthy taste, which works well with autumnal flavours such as apple and walnut. Annie

BEETROOT BIRCHER WITH APPLE + WALNUTS

────────

1. Blitz the beetroot with the apple juice.
2. Place the rest of the ingredients for the Bircher in a mixing bowl and stir to combine.
3. Transfer the beetroot mixture to the bowl and stir. 4. Cover and place in the fridge overnight. 5. The next morning, divide the mixture between 2 bowls. Serve with the suggested toppings.

Makes 2 bowls

Bircher
1 cooked beetroot (beet)
1 tablespoon apple juice
125 g (4 oz/1 cup) oats (oatmeal)
100 ml (3½ fl oz/⅓ cup) coconut
    yoghurt
100 ml (3½ fl oz/⅓ cup) water
½ apple, peeled and grated

Toppings
toasted walnuts
chopped apple

The chilli adds a subtle kick to this Bircher, but it's by no means overpowering as the dense, soaked oats balance out the taste. Annie

ORANGE + GRAPEFRUIT BIRCHER WITH CHILLI

——————

1. To make the grapefruit compote, peel the grapefruit and discard any pith. 2. Segment the grapefruit using a knife to get the juiciest part of the fruit, leaving behind any pith, and reserving the juices. 3. Add to a pan with the juices and bring to the boil with the remaining ingredients. Simmer gently for about 20–30 minutes, then leave to cool. 4. To make the Bircher, place all the ingredients in a mixing bowl and stir to combine. 5. Cover and place in the fridge overnight. 6. The next morning, divide the mixture into 2 bowls. Serve with the grapefruit compote and a sprinkling of toasted flaked almonds and dried chilli flakes.

Makes 2 bowls

Grapefruit compote
2 grapefruit
1 tablespoon honey
1 cm (½ in) piece of fresh ginger,
    peeled and finely chopped
juice of ½ lemon

Bircher
150 ml (5 fl oz/⅔ cup) orange juice
125 g (4 oz/1 cup) oats (oatmeal)
100 ml (3½ fl oz/⅓ cup) natural
    yoghurt

Topping
toasted flaked almonds
dusting of dried chilli flakes

Coconut milk curbs my cravings for something creamy without feeling like I'm over-indulging. I've added maple syrup here, but for those wanting to cut down on sugar, the coconut and vanilla provide enough natural sweetness on their own. Annie

COCONUT +
VANILLA BIRCHER

Makes 2 bowls

Bircher
200 ml (7 fl oz/¾ cup) coconut milk
125 g (4 oz/1 cup) jumbo oats
1 tablespoon chia seeds
1 tablespoon maple syrup
seeds scraped from ½ vanilla pod or
   ½ teaspoon vanilla extract
squeeze of lime

Toppings
coconut chips
sliced banana
blueberries

1. Place all the ingredients for the Bircher in a mixing bowl and stir to combine. 2. Cover and place in the fridge overnight. 3. The next morning, divide the mixture into 2 bowls and serve with the suggested toppings.

SAVOURY

We are both big fans of all things cereal and grains, but
sometimes we crave other things. Sweetness is great on some
days, but on others our taste buds can only be satisfied by
something savoury. For us, this craving comes on those days
when we have a little more time in the mornings to prepare
breakfast from fresh and enjoy the whole process.

These recipes are ones that we love for weekend brunches,
for ourselves and our family and friends. Perfect to make as
you brew up and drink some coffee and tea, catch up on the
news and generally enjoy a more relaxed morning.

MEXICAN
BREAKFAST BOWL

—

I have been a huge fan of Mexican food since my first visit to
California in 1994, where I encountered something so far removed
from what I had previously experienced in London that I could
scarcely believe it was the same cuisine. I love the freshness of the
lime and salsas, as well of the heat of the chillies. This breakfast is a
staple in my house for weekend brunches, especially in the summer.
The smoky taste of the chilli salsa works so well in this dish and is
also very good with other egg dishes. Jonny

1. For the corn salsa, pat the corn kernels dry using paper towels, then place directly into a hot frying pan (skillet) to char. The aim is to get a nice colour on the corn and get a toasted flavour through the salsa. 2. Strip the leaves from the coriander and finely chop them. 3. Once the corn has cooled a little, combine it with the remaining salsa ingredients in a bowl and mix. 4. For the refried beans, melt the butter in a frying pan over a medium heat. Add the onion and garlic and cook for 5–10 minutes until soft. 5. Turn the heat up a little and add the beans, pressing them gently with the back of a spoon. Leave some beans whole and some crushed (unless you prefer a more even texture). If the mixture is getting a little dry, add some stock or cooking liquid to achieve the preferred texture.
6. For the red chilli salsa, start by taking the stalks off the chillies and removing the seeds. 7. Fry the chillies in the oil for a couple of minutes until they are slightly lighter in colour. Remove the chillies and add the halved tomatillos or tomatoes to the pan. 8. Cook for a couple of minutes on both sides and then put them in a blender with the fried chillies, garlic, lime juice, honey and cinnamon. Gradually add the water and pulse until you get the consistency you want. 9. To serve, place a generous portion of the beans and corn salsa next to a sliced half of avocado. Fry an egg, place it on top and drizzle with chilli salsa – the amount depends on how spicy you are feeling that morning.

Makes around 4 generous portions

4 eggs, to serve
2 ripe avocado, peeled, de-stoned
    and cut in half, to serve

Corn salsa

1 × 250 g (9 oz) tin sweetcorn,
    drained (or fresh from the cob)
bunch of fresh coriander (cilantro)
3 medium tomatoes, diced
3 spring onions (scallions), finely
    chopped
juice of 2 limes
2 tablespoons olive oil
1 teaspoon ground cumin

Refried beans

1 tablespoon butter
1 medium onion, peeled and chopped
1 garlic clove, finely chopped
1 × 400 g (14 oz) tin black beans,
    drained (or soaked and cooked
    dried beans)
vegetable stock (or some of the liquid
    reserved from cooking the beans)

Red chilli salsa

16 dried arbol chillies
1 tablespoon olive oil
8 tomatillos (you can use tomatoes if
    you cannot find these), halved
3 garlic cloves, peeled
juice of 1 lime
2 tablespoons honey
pinch of ground cinnamon
250 ml (8½ fl oz/1 cup) water

HERBED COTTAGE CHEESE
WITH POACHED EGGS + PICKLED BEETROOT

———

'I like to get up before anyone else does. I love those quiet hours, when I can prepare the most delicious breakfasts to wake others up with.'

Renée Kemps, food blogger, *Renée Kemps*

Renée's blog was one of the first that I started following very regularly – helped by the fact that when we started up Spoon Cereals, I had just moved back from living in Amsterdam, where she is based. The food and photos in the blog made me nostalgic for the small, artisan shops and cafés that characterise the city. This recipe is, for me, typical of Renée's approach to food – a delicious combination of simple ingredients, prepared well. Jonny

1. Preferably the day (or more) before you want to eat this, mix the cottage cheese with the dill, lemon zest and salt and pepper (to taste). 2. For the quick-pickled beetroot, place the beetroot in a big saucepan and cover with water. Bring to the boil and cook until tender. Peel the skin off and cut them, using a mandoline or sharp knife, into slices 5 mm (¼ in) thick. Place in a big Mason jar, pour over the apple cider vinegar and maple syrup and fill up with water to the rim. Leave the beetroot in a cool place for at least 4 hours, and up to a couple of days. 3. For the Parmesan oil, add the rinds of Parmesan cheese to the oil and simply leave to infuse. The longer, the better. 4. When you are ready to serve, preheat the oven to 110°C (230°F/Gas ¼). 5. Cut the sourdough bread into 2 cm (¾ in) cubes. Place on a baking tray and put in the oven to dry out, for about 10 minutes. Melt the butter in a large pan, add the bread cubes and salt, and toss to coat. Toast until golden brown and crispy. Set aside. 6. Fill a big saucepan with water, bring to the boil and add a little salt. Bring back to a gentle simmer. Crack each egg into a little bowl, one by one, and gently drop them into the simmering water. Depending on the size of your eggs, leave to poach for 3–4 minutes. Remove and place on paper towels to absorb the water. Repeat with the remaining eggs, or cook together if your pan is large enough. 7. To assemble, for each person, take a bowl and place a few spoonfuls of cottage cheese on the bottom. Place a poached egg and a few slices of the pickled beetroot on top. Drizzle with a little Parmesan oil. Add the sourdough croutons, fresh basil and a few sprigs of rocket and serve straight away.

Makes 4 bowls

4 eggs
handful of basil, to serve
rocket (arugula), to serve

Cottage cheese

200 g (7 oz/1 cup) cottage cheese
handful of dill, chopped
zest of ½ lemon
salt and freshly ground black pepper

Quick-pickled beetroot (beets)

1–2 small beetroot (beets)
200 ml (7 fl oz/¾ cup) apple cider
    vinegar (use white wine vinegar
    for a less strong pickle)
1 tablespoon maple syrup

Parmesan oil

1–2 rinds of Parmesan cheese
200 ml (7 fl oz/¾ cup) extra virgin
    olive oil

Sourdough croutons

2 thick slices sourdough bread
2 tablespoons butter
pinch of salt

GREEN
SCRAMBLED EGGS

_____

*'My philosophy is to eat what's in season, and to always eat colourfully!
I love to cook honest, healthy food, which makes me feel great. For me,
embracing the freshest seasonal produce is the simplest way of doing this.'*
Joey O'Hare, private chef and supper club host

Joey's passion for cooking is evident from her many achievements
to date – her background includes helping to run a food start-up
company, making lovely, fresh pesto and appearing on BBC2's hugely
popular *MasterChef: The Professionals*, where she wowed top food
critics with her beautifully simple and delicate dishes. Annie

Makes 1 bowl

knob of butter
2 eggs
bunch of fresh herbs, finely chopped
    (such as mint, flat-leaf parsley,
    tarragon, basil)
small handful of baby spinach, finely
    chopped
½ ripe avocado
salt and freshly ground black pepper

Topping
feta cheese, crumbled
chopped green chilli
olive oil
½ lime

1. In a small pan, melt the butter. Scramble the
eggs, throwing in the chopped soft herbs and
baby spinach halfway through cooking.
2. Peel, stone and chop the avocado, then place
this in the bottom of the bowl. Season to taste.
3. Spoon the scrambled eggs on top and serve
with a little crumbled feta, chopped green chilli,
a drizzle of olive oil, and a squeeze of lime.

VEGGIE BREAKFAST
IN A TACO BOWL

Making your taco bowl from scratch is pretty simple but does take
a bit of time, so in this recipe I've opted for ready-made tortilla wraps.

It took a while to finesse my sweet potato and carrot fritter recipe,
but thanks to family and friends, who've scrutinised every batch I've
made, this recipe is a lovely blend of sweet and spicy flavours. I make
them into a quenelle shape, which can be presented nicely in the bowl,
but flat, rosti-shaped fritters are just as good. Annie

1. Place 3 ovenproof soup bowls on a baking tray. Brush the bowls with a thin layer of oil. 2. Nestle the wraps into the bowls and brush the tops with a thin layer of oil.
3. Bake in the oven for 10 minutes, rotating them after 5 minutes. The wraps should be lightly golden in colour. Once all the bowls are cooked, remove from the oven and set aside. 4. To make the fritters, mix the grated potato and carrots together in a large bowl. Make sure you squeeze out all of the excess water from the mix. Set aside a small bunch of coriander for the garnish and finely chop the remainder. Add the ground coriander, chopped coriander, cumin, chilli, lemon zest and salt to the mix. Leave to stand for 5–10 minutes. 5. Whisk the flour with the baking powder and eggs. Add to the potato mix and combine all the ingredients with your hands. Take about 1 tablespoon of the mix and form into a quenelle or fritter shape. 6. Heat a large frying pan (skillet) over a medium heat and a 5 mm (¼ in) layer of oil. Fry each fritter for about 1 minute on each side until they turn a crispy, golden colour. 7. Place the cooked fritters on a plate lined with kitchen towel, then transfer to a baking tray and put in the oven to keep warm. 8. To make the mushrooms, wipe out the pan and place it over a medium heat. Add the oil. Add the mushrooms and garlic to the pan and cook for 5–10 minutes. 9. Strip the thyme leaves from the stalks and add the leaves to the mushrooms. Season to taste. Cook gently for a further 1–2 minutes. Put the frying pan in the oven (or cover it), to keep the mushrooms warm.
10. Poach the eggs in a pan of water for 3 minutes on a rolling boil. Meanwhile, de-stone and slice the avocado and roughly chop the reserved coriander. 11. Remove the fitters and mushrooms from the oven. 12. When all your components are ready, assemble your bowls by spooning the mushrooms into the taco bowl first, followed by the fritters, poached egg and avocado. Top with the chopped coriander and fresh chilli, if you like, to garnish.

Makes 6 taco bowls

6 × soft tortilla wraps (white or wholemeal)
6 eggs
2 avocados
1 chilli, finely chopped (optional)

Sweet potato fritters

1 large sweet potato, peeled and finely grated
2 carrots, peeled and finely grated
handful of fresh coriander (cilantro)
2 teaspoons ground coriander
2 teaspoons ground cumin
½ teaspoon dried chilli flakes (optional)
zest of 1 lemon
1 teaspoon salt
freshly ground black pepper
3 tablespoons plain (all-purpose) flour
¼ teaspoon baking powder
2 eggs
cooking oil, for shallow frying

Mushrooms

1 tablespoon olive oil
600 g (1 lb 5 oz/7⅓ cups) mushrooms, sliced
3 garlic cloves, finely chopped
8 fresh thyme sprigs
salt and freshly ground black pepper

We first met Adam after serving him a breakfast bowl from our stand at a music festival in Devon. We've remained friends ever since.

'On the weekends I love a savoury breakfast and will often cook a chicken noodle soup, egg-fried rice or kedgeree (that all-time British classic). If my wife cooks a chilli during the week, she will keep some rice for the weekend, which saves on preparation time.'

Adam Byatt, chef and restaurateur

KEDGEREE

---

1. Gently poach the haddock in the milk for 8 minutes. Remove the haddock, reserving the milk. Cover and set aside. 2. Melt the butter in a frying pan (skillet), add the onion and curry powder and cook gently with a little salt until the onion is soft. Add the flour and cook briefly to form a roux. 3. With the pan off the heat, add 1 ladleful of the warm poaching milk to the roux, stirring constantly. Return the pan to a gentle heat and continue to add the milk gradually, stirring all the time. Once the milk has all been incorporated, leave to simmer for 5 minutes. 4. Warm the rice in a steamer, or place briefly in boiling water, then drain. Season to taste. 5. To serve, spoon the rice into 4 bowls. Halve the boiled eggs and place each half in a bowl. Spoon the sauce and flaked smoked haddock into the centre and garnish with chopped coriander and a sprinkling of curry powder.

Makes 4 bowls

300 g (10½ oz) undyed smoked haddock

570 ml (1 pint/2⅓ cups) full-fat (whole) milk

60 g (2 oz/½ stick) butter

1 onion, finely diced

2 teaspoons light curry powder, plus extra to garnish

60 g (2 oz/½ cup) plain (all-purpose) flour

500 g (1 lb 2 oz/2⅔ cups) cooked basmati rice

salt and freshly ground black pepper, to taste

2 eggs, softly boiled for 7 minutes, peeled

small bunch coriander (cilantro), roughly chopped

Dave Gatenby has been a significant pillar of support as we work to grow the Spoon Cereals brand. His love of food stems from spending long summer holidays in Devon cooking communal meals over wood fires and barbecues. As a photographer, he spends his days in the studio cooking and photographing food. To showcase his creativity, he runs a supper club called Banquet in south-west London. Annie

DAVE'S INCREDIBLE BEANS

1. Preheat the oven to 180°C (350°F/Gas 4).
2. Place the butternut squash on a baking tray, add the paprika, 1 tablespoon of the olive oil and some salt and pepper, and toss to coat. Roast for 20 minutes.
3. Meanwhile, sweat the onion and garlic in a frying pan (skillet) with 1 tablespoon olive oil, until soft and golden. Add the red wine vinegar and sugar to the onions, followed by the tomato passata and a splash of water. Bring to a simmer, then add the butter beans and roasted squash. 4. Season the beans with salt and pepper and divide between individual ovenproof bowls. Bake for 30 minutes. 5. Heat a griddle pan up to full whack, then rub the sourdough bread with another tablespoon of olive oil and season with salt. Place on the griddle and cook until crispy and blackened. 7. In the same pan, char the cubes of halloumi until golden brown. 8. Carefully remove the beans from the oven. Add the sourdough slices and halloumi cubes to each bowl and garnish with coriander leaves. A final dusting of paprika at this stage would be perfect.

Makes 4 bowls

1 butternut squash, peeled and chopped into 1 cm (½ in) cubes
1 teaspoon smoked paprika, plus extra to dust
3–4 tablespoons olive oil
salt and freshly ground black pepper
1 red onion, finely diced
3 garlic cloves, finely sliced
2 tablespoons red wine vinegar
pinch of sugar
1 × 700g (1lb 8 oz) jar tomato passata
1 × 400g (14 oz) tin or jar good-quality butter beans, drained
sourdough bread, cut into thick slices
1 x 250 g (4 oz) packet of halloumi, cubed
fresh coriander (cilantro), leaves finely chopped

SMOOTHIES

Smoothies are simple to make, amazingly versatile and a great way to enjoy a mixture of fruit and veg. It's an investment, but having a smoothie maker means endless varieties can be made whenever you feel the need for a little extra health boost. We've put together a few recipes that we like to have first thing in the morning, which can be enjoyed on their own or in the form of a smoothie bowl, finished with your favourite crunchy toppings.

Makes 2 large smoothies

4 medium apples (mixture of red
   and green)
½ lemon
⅓ cucumber
handful of spinach
around 8 mint leaves (to taste)
375 ml (12 fl oz/1½ cups) water
   (or ice equivalent)

1. Core the apples and peel the lemon, then blend all the ingredients together. (There's no need to peel the apples, but do wash them carefully.) 2. This will give you a reasonably thick smoothie, so add a little more water or ice if you wish.

REFRESHING GREEN SMOOTHIE

———

Smoothies are my go-to breakfast on those days when I'm in a rush or when I have been up early and exercising. On both occasions I want something quick, easy and refreshing. This smoothie is a summer favourite, particularly after a morning run, as it tastes so fresh and also gives you immediate rehydration and an energy boost. You can add less water than the recipe suggests, if you prefer a thicker texture. Jonny

Breakfast for me should be eaten like a king, so if it's a smoothie in the morning I like something a little more 'meal-like'. The mango is sherbet-y and refreshing, while tahini and almond milk create a thick, creamy consistency that gives my body the sustenance it needs first thing in the morning. I like to use almond milk from The Pressery. Annie

MANGO + TAHINI SMOOTHIE

_____

Makes 2 smoothies

200 ml (7 fl oz/¾ cup) almond milk
2 bananas, peeled
1 mango, peeled and coarsely
    chopped
juice of 1 lemon
seeds of 1 cardamom pod
2 teaspoons tahini
1 teaspoon ground cinnamon
drizzle of maple syrup (optional)

1. Combine all the ingredients in a blender or smoothie maker. **2.** Add an ice cube, if you like your smoothie extra cold. Drink immediately.

Makes 2 large smoothies

375 ml (12 fl oz/1 ½ cups) milk
    (any kind)
3 bananas, peeled
4–8 dates (depending on their size
    and how sweet your tooth is)
30 g (1 oz/⅓ cup) oats (oatmeal),
    optional
2 teaspoons ground cinnamon

1. Blend all the ingredients together, adding more or less milk, as you like until you reach the consistency desired.

BANANA + DATE SMOOTHIE

———

This has always been one of my favourite smoothies, as it not only tastes delicious (and has many simple variants) but it also gives you all the energy you need until lunch. If you include the optional oats, it's like a raw, smooth porridge.

I like to use oat or almond milk for this. Try substituting the cinnamon with cocoa powder and adding a shot of coffee for a mocha version to really get your morning started with a bit of a kick. Jonny

ACAI BOWL

———

'I love starting my day by having a stretch as soon as I've woken up. It's probably the only thing I can do on an empty stomach — and then I have breakfast to look forward to.'

Elle Landgren, creator of *Elle Fit Active*

I was first introduced to Elle Landgren by my wife, who has used her stretching guides for quite some time now. However hectic or busy my day is, I try to find time to stretch – following this up with a fruit smoothie feels like a natural progression. We've given a list of suggested toppings – simply adapt them according to what's in season. Jonny

1. Blend the ingredients together in a blender or smoothie maker. **2.** Top with your favourite fruit, nuts and seeds or granola.

Makes 2 bowls

250 ml (8½ fl oz/1 cup) almond milk or coconut water
150 g (5 oz/1 cup) frozen strawberries
150 g (5 oz/1 cup) frozen blueberries
2 heaped teaspoons acai powder
1 banana, peeled

Toppings
fruit, such as strawberries, blueberries, banana, kiwi fruit, passion fruit
nuts and seeds
favourite granola

My banana-flavoured yoghurt recipe always went down really well during our market and pop-up trading days. It forms the base of a morning breakfast bowl that can be topped with your favourite seasonal fruits, nuts and seeds. In this recipe I have toasted the nuts for a more wholesome flavour. I like to toast them in large batches and save for hectic weekday mornings. Any kind of natural yoghurt works for this recipe. Be aware that low-fat yoghurt will create a thinner consistency. Annie

BANANA YOGHURT BOWL

——————

1. Preheat the oven to 180°C (350°F/Gas 4).
2. Place the hazelnuts onto a baking tray and bake for 15–20 minutes, until they turn a light shade of brown and the skins start to peel.
3. Blend the bananas, yoghurt and apple juice together until they form a smooth consistency.
4. Remove the hazelnuts from the oven and leave to cool. 5. Pour the banana mixture into your favourite bowls. Sprinkle with your preferred amount of cacao nibs and hazelnuts.

Makes 2 bowls

200 g (7 oz/1¼ cup) hazelnuts (makes a large batch for multiple bowls), roughly chopped
2 large bananas, peeled
200 ml (7 fl oz) natural yoghurt
2 tablespoons apple juice
10 g (½ oz) cacao nibs

BREAKFAST ACCOMPANIMENTS

———

We've called this section Breakfast Accompaniments because we feel breakfast wouldn't be complete without these recipes. From delicious cookies and stewed fruits to a selection of butters to spread on toast or add to your breakfast bowl, these are great additions to your morning. We particularly love the butters for their naturally sweet and sticky caramel-like consistency, which is a welcome energy-boosting treat, drizzled on top of your porridge as well as your toast in the morning.

Thanks to my Canadian roots, I was introduced to maple syrup at an early age. Maple syrup wasn't widely available in the UK in the 1980s, making its fantastic taste highly desirable. Now that it is easier to get hold of I was really pleased to learn of a great way to intensify the maple taste of the syrup even further and make it more spreadable. Enter Maple Butter – a creamier, thicker version of maple syrup that helps make breakfasts and snack time even more exciting. Jonny

MAPLE BUTTER

1. Prepare an ice bath: take a bowl, large enough to fit a second, smaller bowl inside, and half-fill it with ice cubes. 2. Pour the maple syrup into a saucepan and heat to 112°C (234°F). (Use a sugar thermometer to check this.) Be very careful when handling the hot syrup and do not be tempted to taste it while hot, as it can cause a very nasty burn. 3. Once the syrup has reached the correct temperature, pour it carefully into the second, smaller mixing bowl and put the bowl in the ice bath. 4. Cool the syrup down to around 16°C (61°F). Once it has reached this temperature, remove the maple syrup from the ice bath and let it warm back up to room temperature. 5. Once the syrup is at room temperature, slowly stir it (either by hand using a whisk, or a mixer fitted with a paddle attachment on slow speed) for up to 30 minutes. It will become lighter and thicker as you persevere with the stirring. The butter is ready when it is the colour and texture of tahini. 6. Pour into a small jar, cover and keep for up to 6 months in the fridge.

Makes 500 ml (17 fl oz/2 cups)

ice cubes (enough to make an ice bath in a mixing bowl)
500 ml (17 fl oz/2 cups) maple syrup

CHAI-POACHED PEARS

——————

'Eat what makes you feel good, whatever that might be.'
Issy Croker, food and lifestyle photographer

Issy was an important part of our first launch event, where she gave an inspiring class in food photography. The chai gives a unique take on these poached pears, which Issy recommends with our Cinnamon + Pecan granola (page 25).

1. In a small, deep saucepan, bring the water to the boil. Remove from the heat, add the tea bags and cinnamon stick and leave to infuse for 10 minutes. 2. Remove the tea bags, squeezing them firmly, so they release as much of their flavour as possible into the water. Stir in the maple syrup. 3. Add the peeled pears (the water should cover them) and bring the water back to a gentle simmer. Poach the pears for 20–25 minutes, or until soft. 4. When soft, remove the pears together with the cinnamon stick and put to one side. Bring the poaching liquid to a rolling boil and simmer for 15–20 minutes until it thickens and goes syrupy. 5. To serve, spoon the yoghurt generously between 3 shallow bowls. Place a poached pear in the middle of each bowl, pour over some of the reduced poaching syrup and sprinkle with your choice of granola to finish.

Makes 3 bowls

350 ml (12 fl oz/1 ⅓ cups) water
3 chai tea bags
1 cinnamon stick
4 tablespoons maple syrup
3 ripe pears, peeled
100 ml (3 ½ fl oz/⅓ cup) Greek
    yoghurt
favourite granola, for sprinkling

I would be lying if I said that all I ate for breakfast was granola. Sometimes a slice of toast (wholemeal or rye) in the morning, piled high with fresh and chunky avocado, a squeeze of lemon, salt and dusting of chilli is a nice way to balance out my weekly breakfast meals. Here are a few other toast-topper ideas, which work just as well for lunch. Annie

THINGS ON TOAST

BAKED BEANS

Serves 2–4

1 tablespoon rapeseed or olive oil
1 garlic clove, finely chopped
1 red onion, finely chopped
1 × 400g (14 oz) tin cannellini beans
1 × 400g (14 oz) tin chopped
  tomatoes
½ teaspoon dried chilli flakes
1 teaspoon finely chopped rosemary
1 bay leaf
1 tablespoon tomato purée
salt and freshly ground black pepper

1. Heat the oil in a pan, add the garlic and onion and cook until soft. 2. Add the rest of the ingredients to the pan and simmer for 20–30 minutes. Season with salt and pepper to taste.

PEANUT BUTTER

Makes 500 g (1 lb 2 oz/3⅓ cups)

500 g (1 lb 2 oz/3⅓ cups) peanuts
1 tablespoon coconut oil
pinch salt

1. Preheat the oven to 180°C (350°F/Gas 4).
2. Place the peanuts on a baking tray and toast for 15 minutes, shaking the tray after 5 minutes to ensure they toast evenly, then remove and leave to cool. 3. Melt the coconut oil in a pan over a medium heat. 4. Blend the toasted peanuts in a food processor or blender for up to 5 minutes, adding the coconut oil bit by bit, until you reach the desired consistency. 5. Store in an airtight, sterilised jar. It will keep for up to 6 months.

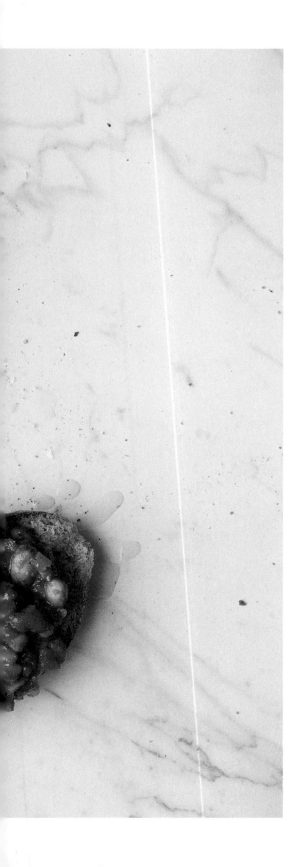

AVOCADO HUMMUS

Serves 2–4

1 × 400 g (14 oz) tin chickpeas
  (garbanzo), drained
125 g (4 oz/¾ cup) frozen peas
75 ml (2 ½ fl oz/¼ cup) olive oil
½ ripe avocado
10 basil leaves
zest and juice of 1 lime
1 garlic clove
2 teaspoons tahini

1. Blend all the ingredients together until you
have a smooth consistency.

DATE JAM

Makes 200 g (7 oz/1 ¼ cups)

200 g (7 oz/1 ¼ cups) pitted
  medjool dates
100 ml (3 ½ fl oz/scant ½ cup)
  water
juice of ½ lemon
1 tablespoon maple syrup (optional)

1. Place the dates in a saucepan with the rest of
the ingredients. 2. Bring to the boil and simmer
for 20 minutes. Take off the heat and leave to
cool. 3. Store your jam in a sterilised jar. This
will keep for up to 6 months in the fridge.

I first stumbled across Zoe Hannam's Minor Goods at a street food market in south London. Zoe believes less is more when it comes to cooking and flavour combinations. Founded by freelance journalist, Miranda York, Druid Street market is full of diverse offerings featuring up-and-coming food producers and hand-made goods. Annie

'It's the minor things in life that can make the difference — enjoying those small everyday details, such as a hand-carved spoon for your sugar or a vintage bowl for your cereal. You only need a few good things to lift your spirits.'

Zoe Hannam, Minor Goods Ceramics

STEWED RHUBARB

1. Wash the rhubarb, then cut into 2.5 cm (1 in) pieces. 2. Place in a saucepan with the remaining ingredients. 3. Cover and cook over a low heat for about 10 minutes, stirring occasionally, until the rhubarb has softened but is still in chunks. 4. When it's ready, drain some of the excess syrup and serve in bowls with your favourite granola, if you like, and natural yoghurt. 5. The syrup can be used as a delicious cordial with sparkling water or added to your favourite smoothie. Store in a sterilised jar in the fridge. It will keep for 5 days.

Makes 2–3 bowls

2 rhubarb stalks
2 tablespoons maple syrup
zest and juice of 1 small orange
½–1 teaspoon ground cinnamon
   (or more, to taste)

Toppings
favourite granola (optional)
natural yoghurt

CINNAMON BUTTER

——————

'My Danish grandmother taught me this amazing recipe when I was a child and it remains one of my favourite guilty pleasures.'

Stine Dulong, ceramicist and founder of SkandiHus

Stine's Scandinavian roots can be seen in her beautiful handmade and natural ceramics. Her talent has been recognised by top chefs such as Jamie Oliver and Tom Kerridge, who have featured her pieces in their own cookbooks and Instagram accounts. We were thrilled that Stine agreed to support this project. You will spot some of her work throughout this book.

1. Beat the butter, brown sugar and cinnamon together in a bowl (you can use an electric mixer, but it's not necessary), until smooth and creamy. 2. This will keep for 6 months (possibly more) in the fridge.

100 g (3 ½ oz/1 stick) butter
60 g (2 oz/⅓ cup, lightly packed) soft brown sugar
1 teaspoon ground cinnamon

TRAIL MIXES

——————

I like to keep my breakfasts unpredictable. These trail-mix combinations are a great way to vary breakfast bowl toppings. If time isn't on your side, these are great to bring with you when you're running out the door. Making big batches means you're sorted for the week. Annie

LEMON, COCONUT + PISTACHIO

1. Preheat the oven to 180°C (350°F/Gas 4).
2. In a bowl, combine all the ingredients, mixing well to coat. Spread out on a baking tray.
3. Place in the oven for 15 minutes, shaking halfway through.   4. Store in an airtight container. It will keep at room temperature for up to a week.

Makes 300 g (10½ oz/1½ cups)

100 g (3½ oz/1 cup) coconut flakes
100 g (3½ oz/⅔ cup) chopped almonds
100 g (3½ oz/⅔ cup) pistachios
zest of ½ lemon, plus 1 teaspoon lemon juice
1 tablespoon honey

DATE, HAZELNUT + CACAO NIBS

1. Preheat the oven to 180°C (350°F/Gas 4).
2. Roughly chop the hazelnuts, place on a baking tray and roast for 10 minutes until lightly toasted. Leave to cool.   3. In a bowl, combine the apple juice and dates. Add the cooled, toasted hazelnuts and the cacao nibs.   4. Store in an airtight container. It will keep at room temperature for up to a week.

Makes 250 g (9 oz/2 cups)

100 g (3½ oz/¾ cup) hazelnuts
1 tablespoon apple juice
100 g (3½ oz/½ cup) chopped dates
2 tablespoons (40 g/1½ oz/¼ cup) cacao nibs

GRANOLA + SEED MIX

1. Preheat the oven to 180°C (350°F/Gas 4).
2. Roughly chop the pecans, place on a baking tray and roast for 10 minutes. Leave to cool.
3. Mix the cooled, toasted pecans with the remaining ingredients.   4. Store in an airtight container. It will keep at room temperature for up to a week.

Makes 400 g (14 oz/3 cups)

60 g (2 oz/½ cup) pecan nuts
100 g (3½ oz/¾ cup) Cinnamon + Pecan granola (see page 25)
60 g (2 oz/½ cup) sunflower seeds
60 g (2 oz/½ cup) pumpkin seeds
60 g (2 oz/½ cup) dried cranberries
1 tablespoon sesame seeds
1 tablespoon linseeds

Natasha Kelly has applied the skills gained while working for several American global fashion brands to her own tea bar. Tiosk, with its simple, clean interior and modern vegan menu, inhabits a small corner of the famous Broadway Market in east London.

'I usually sneak out of bed at around 6 or 6.30 a.m. before my four children arise, dodging the creaky floorboards in order not to wake them. I find that this is the only truly peaceful time in each day and it allows me to get work done that requires real focus and head space.'

Natasha Kelly, founder and owner of Tiosk

TEA-SOAKED FIGS

1. Put the Lapsang Souchong into a teapot or heatproof jug (you can make a little muslin sack if you prefer). Pour the boiling water over the leaves and allow to steep for 5 minutes. **2.** Halve the figs and place in a clean glass jar.
3. Add the cardamom pods and Himalayan pink salt.
4. Slit the vanilla pod open lengthways, exposing the seeds, and loosen them with the tip of the knife. Place the whole pod into the jar with the figs and the cardamom.
5. Strain the leaves from the brewed Lapsang Souchong (or remove the muslin bag), reserving the brewed tea.
6. Pour the tea over the figs, vanilla and cardamom, seal the jar and store in the fridge overnight. Your infused figs will last for 5–7 days if kept refrigerated.

Serves 4

2 tablespoons Lapsang Souchong
   or 3 tea bags
1 litre (34 fl oz/4 cups) boiling water
8 fresh figs (black or green)
3 green cardamom pods
tiny pinch of Himalayan pink salt
1 vanilla pod

250 ml (8 fl oz/1 cup) unsweetened
   almond milk
100 g (3 ½ oz/¾ cup) oats
   (oatmeal)
2 tablespoons chia seeds

Toppings
almond butter (creamy or crunchy)
sliced banana
toasted sliced almonds
Tea-Soaked Figs (page 128)

1. Place all the ingredients in a mixing bowl
and stir to combine. **2.** Cover and place in the
fridge overnight. **3.** The next morning, divide
the mixture into bowls. Serve with the suggested
toppings.

CHIA BIRCHER

———

Kit + Ace is a lifestyle and technical luxury fashion label. Recognised
across the globe, each individual store connects creatives in their
local community. I was introduced to the east London branch through
a chef friend of mine and have since gone to supply granola to their
breakfast events and attended intimate, monthly supper clubs. Thanks
to co-founder JJ Wilson for this recipe. Annie

BREAKFAST MUFFINS + COOKIES

Living in balance to us means enjoying those little everyday luxuries as well as feeding our bodies with plenty of whole foods, fruit and vegetables and staying active. Great for feeding a crowd, none of these breakfast muffins or cookies lasted very long on our cookbook shoot!
Annie + Jonny

1. BREAKFAST MUFFINS

Architect Chris and designer Tom are responsible for our new pop-up bar that we take to creative morning-time events.

'If we were to describe our studio in food terms it would have to be something good for sharing, unfussy and uncomplicated — something easy to consume when we gather around a table to have a brainstorm for a project. It would have to be delicious and substantial. These muffins seem to tick all the boxes and are perfect for a morning team-briefing session or a breakfast meeting. They are filling, thanks to the bran and oats, and moist because of the soaked prunes.

They are also great for making in batches at the weekend and then enjoying as a speedy breakfast during the week — they keep well for a good few days. They are also suitable for freezing. Wrap the freshly baked muffins individually before freezing. If you want to enjoy a muffin for breakfast, take it out of the freezer in the evening and leave at room temperature overnight.'

Chris Kennedy and Tom Woods of
Kennedy Woods Architecture

1. Preheat the oven to 170°C (340°F/Gas 3) and line a muffin tin with paper cases. 2. Put the Earl Grey tea bag in a small bowl and pour over the boiling water. Allow to soak for a few minutes. Place the prunes in the bowl. 3. Melt the butter with the sugar in a small saucepan. Set aside to cool slightly. 4. Heat a large frying pan (skillet) and toast the almonds for a few minutes until lightly browned and fragrant – keep a close eye on them as they can burn quickly. Transfer to a chopping board and set aside to cool. 5. Put the flour, oats, oat bran, salt and bicarbonate of soda in a large bowl and mix well. Roughly chop the toasted almonds and add them to the mix. 6. Take the prunes out of their tea bowl and chop into bite-sized pieces. 7. In a bowl, whisk the eggs and the yoghurt, add the butter and sugar mix and stir in the prunes. Pour all this over the dry ingredients and mix until just combined. Avoid stirring the dough too much, otherwise the muffins could turn out hard. 8. Spoon equal quantities of the mixture into the muffin cases. Sprinkle with some oats and bake for 20–25 minutes, until fully risen and golden in colour.

Makes 12

1 Earl Grey tea bag
150–200 ml (5–7 fl oz/½–¾ cup) boiling water (exact quantity is not crucial here)
250 g (9 oz/1 cup) soft prunes
200 g (7 oz/1¾ sticks) unsalted butter
75 g (2½ oz/⅓ cup, lightly packed) soft light brown sugar
100 g (3½ oz/⅔ cup) whole almonds, skins on
200 g (7 oz/1⅓ cups) wholemeal spelt flour
100 g (3½ oz/¾ cup) oats (oatmeal), plus extra for sprinkling
150 g (5 oz/2 cups) oat bran
½ teaspoon salt
1½ teaspoons bicarbonate of soda (baking soda)
2 eggs
350 ml (11 fl oz/1⅓ cups) natural yoghurt

I was first welcomed into Anna Jones' beautiful east London home for a cup of tea when Spoon Cereals was at its humble beginnings. At the time, Anna was making waves with her first cookbook, *A Modern Way to Eat* (HarperCollins, 2014), which is our go-to cookbook when we crave a healthy veggie meal. Annie

'A few years back, I told myself that I deserved a real breakfast every morning. Whether that's sitting on my back doorstep, enjoying a cup of coffee and watching the early sun break through my beloved mimosa tree, or hurriedly eating a delicious bowl of granola before rushing out of the door; somehow breakfast for me is setting out my intention of how I want the day to be.'

Anna Jones, cook, food writer and stylist

2. LEMON + ORANGE MILLET COOKIES

1. Preheat the oven to 180°C (350°F/Gas 4). Line a baking sheet with baking parchment. 2. Zest both lemons and juice one. Combine the olive oil, yoghurt, lemon juice, half the lemon zest and the orange zest in a bowl.
3. In a separate bowl, mix all the dry ingredients. Pour the wet ingredients into the dry and mix until you have a soft, doughy consistency. If it's too dry, add a little more yoghurt.
4. Roll the dough into 20 evenly sized balls, then place on the prepared baking sheet and press down lightly to flatten. Sprinkle with the extra millet flakes and coconut, and the remaining lemon zest. 5. Bake for 10–15 minutes, until golden. The biscuits will be soft when they come out, but will firm up as they cool.

Makes about 20

Wet ingredients
2 lemons
125 ml (4 fl oz/½ cup) olive oil
4 tablespoons natural yoghurt
zest of 1 orange

Dry ingredients
165 g (5½ oz/1¼ cups) white spelt
  flour
125 g (4 oz/⅔ cup, lightly packed)
  soft light brown or coconut sugar
75 g (2½ oz/⅔ cup) oats (oatmeal)
40 g (1½ oz/⅓ cup) millet flakes,
  plus extra to top
40 g (1½ oz/½ cup) unsweetened
  desiccated coconut, plus extra,
  to top

3. WALNUT, CRANBERRY + COURGETTE MUFFINS

Camilla Ferarro is a self-taught, 'messy' cook, nutritionist and dietetic Master's student based in Melbourne, Australia, who loves nothing more than pottering about in the kitchen producing wholesome meals and treats that are nutritious, yet equally delicious. She is passionate about inspiring others to rekindle their connection with food. Where does it come from? How is it produced? What does it contain? She believes that home cooking, eating real, whole, seasonal foods – and the occasional piece of cake for breakfast – are key to achieving good health and vitality.

Serve these loaves with some luscious Greek yoghurt and seasonal fresh or poached fruit for a wholesome and satisfying breakfast. For a little extra deliciousness, replace some or all of the dried cranberries in this recipe with dark chocolate chips (or chopped dark chocolate). Adding finely grated lemon zest to the batter also works a treat.

'In my book, eating cake for breakfast is entirely acceptable, especially when it has been lovingly homemade. These breakfast loaves strike the perfect balance, being delicately sweet and wholesome, whilst avoiding the richness and ensuing sugar coma from a full-blown piece of cake first thing in the morning.'

Camilla Ferarro,
food blogger, *The Alimental Sage*

1. Preheat the oven to 180°C (350°F/Gas 4) and thoroughly grease an 8-hole mini loaf tin or a 12-hole muffin tin. 2. In a large mixing bowl, combine the buckwheat flour, ground almonds, spices, vanilla, baking powder, bicarbonate of soda, walnuts and cranberries. 3. In a separate bowl, whisk together the eggs, maple syrup and olive oil. Add the wet ingredients to the dry and gently mix to combine, before carefully folding through the grated courgette. 4. The moisture content of your courgettes will vary, so if the batter appears far too wet then add in a little extra buckwheat flour. Alternatively, drizzle in a touch more olive oil, if it appears too dry. 5. Carefully spoon the mixture into the prepared tin, filling each hole about two-thirds full (it can help to use an ice cream scoop for easy distribution). Bake in the oven for 20–25 minutes, or until a skewer inserted into the centre of the cakes comes out clean. 6. Allow the muffins to cool in the pan for at least 5–10 minutes before gently removing and allowing to cool further on a wire rack. 7. Serve the muffins warm or cool. They will keep well for 2–4 days, and also freeze well.

Makes 8 mini loaves or 12 medium muffins

butter, for greasing
190 g (6½ oz/1½ cups) unpeeled grated courgette (zucchini), firmly packed and squeezed of moisture

Dry ingredients

100 g (3½ oz/¾ cup) buckwheat flour
100 g (3½ oz/1 cup) ground almonds
1½ heaped teaspoons ground cinnamon
¼ teaspoon ground nutmeg
¼ teaspoon vanilla bean powder or extract
1 teaspoon baking powder
½ teaspoon bicarbonate of soda (baking soda)
60 g (2 oz/⅔ cup) walnut halves, roughly chopped
40 g (½ oz/⅓ cup) dried cranberries, roughly chopped

Wet ingredients

3 large eggs
125 ml (4 fl oz/½ cup) maple syrup
60 ml (2 fl oz/¼ cup) olive oil

Makes 1 jar

200 g (7 oz/1 cup) peanuts
200 g (7 oz/1 cup) Cinnamon +
    Pecan Granola (page 25), or any
    granola of your choice
1 tablespoon coconut oil, melted
    or peanut oil, plus extra if required

1. Preheat the oven to 180°C (350°F/Gas 4).
2. Place the peanuts on a baking tray and place in the oven for 15 mins. Remove and leave to cool. 3. Blend the granola and roasted peanuts for up to 5 minutes, adding oil little by little, until you reach the consistency you are happy with.
4. If you like an even smoother texture, add an extra teaspoon of oil.

GRANOLA BUTTER

―――――

Nut butters are so easy to make at home. Simply choose your favourite nut, roast it, season a little, then whizz the hell out of it in a blender until you reach your desired consistency. Turns out the same can be done for granola. You can add a little extra oil to this recipe, to loosen up the texture – the result is a gooey granola butter that can be enjoyed on top of porridge or as an energy-lifting snack with fresh apple. If you're using coconut oil, melt it gently in a pan first. Annie

ABOUT THE AUTHORS

JONNY SHIMMIN currently lives and works in London, where he grew up.
Prior to setting up Spoon Cereals with Annie, he lived in both London and
Amsterdam, where he worked in investment. After far too much time spent
thinking about working for himself, he is very happy to finally be doing so.

ANNIE MORRIS graduated in Graphic and Communication Design and has
a Master's in Advertising and Design from the University of Leeds. After
working as part of a creative duo in the advertising industry in central
London for two years, she decided to test her idea for London's first breakfast
cereal pop-up bar. She's not looked back.

THANK YOU

Since starting Spoon Cereals we have built a habit of going into the
unknown. This was certainly the case with this cookbook and we would like
to thank everyone who has worked with us to make this possible, especially:

   All at Hardie Grant, especially Kajal Mistry and Kate Pollard. Support
above and beyond the call of duty.

Jacqui Melville – for your sublime photography skills.

Clare Skeats – for such simple, elegant design.

Lily Simpson – for kindly loaning your beautiful space to us.

All of our incredible contributors – you keep us inspired and we have no doubt that you will have the same impact on everyone who reads this book.

Hugh and Dave – such generous and talented guys.

Helena and Rasa – we are so grateful for all your creative input.

Deborah and Peter – for backing us right at the start.

ANNIE

Jonny – your laid-back and relaxed attitude to whatever life throws your way has been a big inspiration to me.

My parents – thank you for putting up with me living at home and filling the basement with Spoon Cereals paraphernalia.

Sarah – my amazing eldest sister, who first introduced me to Jonny. An honorary Spoon Cereals team member.

Pips – I am very lucky to have you as not just a sister, but a mentor too.

G dog – your passion for what you do has been a big inspiration.

Leo and Helen – you are the best ambassadors we could have wished for.

All my awesome friends – thanks for understanding, guys. You know who you are. Special mention to Jessy for helping us work towards our new product launch. Also, Ed Haslam and Harry Trussell.

Finally to Matt, who has always been there from the beginning despite having enough on his plate. Thanks for being my rock.

JONNY

Sarah – I hope someday to be able to repay the extensive love, patience and support that you have given me. I look forward to having all the time in the world to make this repayment!

Mum – Recipe-tester extraordinaire; we are very grateful for all of your help in putting the book together.

My sisters, Pippa, Cathy and Annie and their families – you have all been as generous as you could with time, moral support and contacts, which was much needed in the early days and still appreciated now.

My business partner Annie – you get both the best and worst of me and so for any particularly grumpy times I apologise! All credit to you for how lovely this book looks.

To all others who have helped in even the smallest way with the growth of Spoon Cereals and the publication of the book – thank you so much.

CONTRIBUTORS + SUPPLIERS

Hugh Johnson Photographer, www.hughjohnson.co.uk

Anna Pinder Food stylist and recipe developer, @annapinder

Jacqueline Skott Co-owner of Snaps + Rye, www.snapsandrye.com

Agnes Gallhägen Food blogger, *Cashew Kitchen,* www.cashew-kitchen.com

Renée Kemps Food blogger, *Renée Kemps,* www.reneekemps.com

Joey O'Hare Private Chef and Supper Club Host

Adam Byatt Chef and Restauranter

David Gatenby Photographer and Super Club Host, @joeyscooking

Elle Landgren Creator of *Elle Fit Active,* www.ellefitactive.com

Issy Croaker Food Photographer and lifestyle photographer, www.issycroker.com, @issycroaker

Zoe Hannam Founder of Minor Goods Ceramics, www.minorgoods.com

Stine Delong Ceramicist and founder of SkandiHus, www.skandihus.co.uk

Natasha Kelly Founder and Owner of the café Tiosk, www.tiosk.co.uk

Chris Kennedy and **Tom Woods** Founders of Kennedy Woods Architecture, www.kennedywoods.co.uk

Anna Jones Cook, food writer and stylist, www.annajones.co.uk

Camilla Ferarro Food Blogger, *The Alimental Sage,* www.camillaferarro.com

Helena La Petite, Lifestyle photographer, www.newfoundpress.com

J G Pottery www.jgpottery.co.uk, @jimbus

Jess Jos www.jessjos.com, @jessjos

Andrea Roman www.arceramics.co.uk, @busanosicoloco

Jono Smart www.jonosmart.co.uk, @jonosmart

MUD Australia www.uk.mudaustralia.com, @mudaustraliainstagram

Dinosaur Designs www.dinosaurdesigns.co.uk, @dinosaur_designs

Maitland and Poate www.maitlandandpoate.com, @maitlandandpoate

Elliott Ceramics www.elliottceramics.com, @elliottceramics

Nina+Co www.ninaand.co, @ninaandcodesign

Daisy Cooper Ceramics www.daisycooperceramics.com, @daisycooperceramics

Kana London www.kanalondon.com, @kanalondon

Minor Goods www.minorgoods.com, @minorgoods

Brickett Davda www.brickettdavda.com, @brickettdavda

Bison Home www.bisonhome.com, @bisonhome

Snaps + Rye www.snapsandrye.com, @snapsandrye

love it want it buy it www.loveitwantitbuyit.co.uk, @loveitwantitbuyit

SkandiHus www.skandihus.co.uk, @skandihus_london

Anna Jones Ceramics www.annajonesceramics.com, @annajonesceramics

Jook www.itsajook.com, @itsajook

Revive Joinery www.revivejoinery.co.uk, @ReviveJoinery

Emma Lacey www.emmalacey.com, @emmalaceyeveryday

Ginger Whisk www.gingerwhisk.com, @gingerwhiskprops

Sarah Schembri Ceramics www.sarahschembri.com, @sarahschembri_ceramics

Lisa Ommanney Ceramics @_lisaomm_ceramics_

Sue Pryke www.suepryke.com, @suepryke

Dassie Artisan www.dassie.co.uk, @dassie_artisan

A

acai bowl 112
accompaniments 117
  avocado hummus 123
  baked beans 121
  breakfast muffins 131–2
  chai-poached pears 120
  cinnamon butter 126
  date jam 123
  granola butter 136
  lemon + orange millet cookies 133
  maple butter 119
  peanut butter 121
  stewed rhubarb 124
  tea-soaked figs 128–9
  trail mixes 126–7
  walnut, cranberry + courgette
    muffins 134–5
almond milk
  green apple Bircher with
    pistachios 81
  mango + tahini smoothie 109
  tea-soaked figs 128–9
almonds
  banana porridge with almonds +
    amaretti 68
  breakfast muffins 131–2
  chocolate + lime granola 37
  homemade bran flakes 52
  lemon + caraway granola with
    peach compote 30–1
  mountain muesli 54
  toasted lemon + ginger muesli 44
amaranth: light lentil granola 26–7
amaretti biscuits: banana porridge
  with almonds + amaretti 68
apples
  beetroot Bircher with apple +
    walnuts 82
  blackberry + apple Bircher 77
  green apple Bircher with
    pistachios 81
  refreshing green smoothie 106
apricots, dried
  summer muesli 49
  three-grain muesli 55
  toasted lemon + ginger muesli 44

avocados
  avocado hummus 123
  avocado porridge with sweet
    chilli 67
  avocado with savoury granola
    crunch 35
  green scrambled eggs 96–7
  Mexican breakfast bowl 90–1
  veggie breakfast in a taco
    bowl 98–9

B

bananas
  acai bowl 112
  banana + date smoothie 111
  banana porridge with almonds +
    amaretti 68
  banana + walnut granola 36
  banana yoghurt bowl 114
  granola ice cream sandwich 40
  mango + tahini smoothie 109
  mountain muesli 54
  rye + oat porridge with kiwi +
    banana chips 62
  tea-soaked figs 128–9
beetroot
  beetroot Bircher with apple +
    walnuts 82
  herbed cottage cheese with
    poached eggs + pickled
    beetroot 94–5
  savoury porridge with lemon-
    roasted fennel, beetroot chips,
    basil oil + sunflower
    'Parmesan' 70–3
berries, autumn: buttermilk
  porridge 60
berries, freeze-dried
  muesli + granola mix 47
  toasted buckwheat with cranberries
    + freeze-dried berries 50
berries, summer: breakfast tiramisu
  39
Bircher 17, 75
  beetroot Bircher with apple +
    walnuts 82
  blackberry + apple Bircher 77

  coconut + vanilla Bircher 87
  green apple Bircher with
    pistachios 81
  orange + grapefruit Bircher with
    chilli 85
  spiced carrot Bircher 78
black beans: Mexican breakfast
  bowl 90–1
blackberry + apple Bircher 77
blueberries
  acai bowl 112
  three-grain muesli 55
  toasted buckwheat with cranberries
    + freeze-dried berries 50
bran flakes, homemade 52
Brazil nuts
  mountain muesli 54
  muesli + granola mix 47
  summer muesli 49
buckwheat flakes
  mountain muesli 54
  summer muesli 49
buckwheat groats: toasted buckwheat
  with cranberries + freeze-dried
  berries 50
butter
  cinnamon butter 126
  granola butter 136
  maple butter 119
butter beans: Dave's incredible
  beans 102
buttermilk porridge 60
butternut squash: Dave's incredible
  beans 102

C

cacao nibs: date, hazelnut + cacao
  nibs trail mix 127
cannellini beans: baked beans
  121
caraway seeds: lemon + caraway
  granola with peach compote 30–1
carrots: spiced carrot Bircher 78
cashew nuts
  avocado with savoury granola
    crunch 35
  toasted buckwheat with cranberries

+ freeze-dried berries 50
chai-poached pears 120
cherries
    Black Forest granola with cherry
        yoghurt + cherry compote
        28–9
    cherry compote 28–9
    cherry yoghurt 28–9
chia seeds
    coconut + vanilla Bircher 87
    tea-soaked figs 128–9
chickpeas: avocado hummus 123
chilli flakes: orange + grapefruit
    Bircher with chilli 85
chillies, red
    avocado porridge with sweet
        chilli 67
    red chilli salsa 90–1
chocolate + lime granola 37
cinnamon
    cinnamon butter 126
    cinnamon + pecan granola 25
coconut
    coconut + vanilla Bircher 87
    lemon, coconut + pistachio trail
        mix 127
coconut milk
    coconut + vanilla Bircher 87
    rye + oat porridge with kiwi +
        banana chips 62
coffee, maple + walnut porridge
    58
compotes
    blackberry + apple Bircher 77
    buttermilk porridge 60
    cherry compote 28–9
    orange + grapefruit Bircher with
        chilli 85
    orange, marmalade + thyme
        compote 64
    peach compote 30–1
cookies: lemon + orange millet
    cookies 133
cottage cheese: herbed cottage
    cheese with poached eggs +
    pickled beetroot 94–5
courgettes: walnut, cranberry +

courgette muffins 134–5
cranberries
    granola + seed mix 127
    light lentil granola 26–7
    toasted buckwheat with cranberries
        + freeze-dried berries 50
    walnut, cranberry + courgette
        muffins 134–5
cucumber: refreshing green
    smoothie 106

D
dates
    banana + date smoothie 111
    date, hazelnut + cacao nibs trail
        mix 127
    date jam 123
    three-grain muesli 55

E
eggs
    breakfast tiramisu 39
    green scrambled eggs 96–7
    herbed cottage cheese with
        poached eggs + pickled
        beetroot 94–5
    kedgeree 101
    Mexican breakfast bowl 90–1
    veggie breakfast in a taco
        bowl 98–9

F
fennel: savoury porridge with
    lemon-roasted fennel, beetroot
    chips, basil oil + sunflower
    'Parmesan' 70–3
feta cheese: green scrambled
    eggs 96–7
figs
    mountain muesli 54
    tea-soaked figs 128–9
fritters: sweet potato fritters 98–9

G
ginger: toasted lemon + ginger
    muesli 44
granola 21, 23

avocado with savoury granola
    crunch 35
banana + walnut granola 36
Black Forest granola with cherry
    yoghurt + cherry compote 28–9
breakfast tiramisu 39
chocolate + lime granola 37
cinnamon + pecan granola 25
granola butter 136
granola ice cream sandwich 40
granola + seed mix 127
honey + thyme granola with natural
    yoghurt + blood orange 32
lemon + caraway granola with
    peach compote 30–1
light lentil granola 26–7
muesli + granola mix 47
grapefruit: orange + grapefruit Bircher
    with chilli 85

H
haddock: kedgeree 101
hazelnuts: date, hazelnut + cacao nibs
    trail mix 127
herbed cottage cheese with poached
    eggs + pickled beetroot 94–5
honey
    honey + thyme granola with natural
        yoghurt + blood orange 32
    sweet chilli jam 67
hummus: avocado hummus 123

I
ice cream: granola ice cream
    sandwich 40

J
jam
    date jam 123
    sweet chilli jam 67

K
kedgeree 101
kiwi fruit: rye + oat porridge with kiwi
    + banana chips 62

L
lemons

lemon + caraway granola with
    peach compote 30–1
lemon + coconut + pistachio trail
    mix 127
lemon, orange millet cookies 133
savoury porridge with lemon-
    roasted fennel, beetroot chips,
    basil oil + sunflower
    'Parmesan' 70–3
toasted lemon + ginger muesli 44
lentils: light lentil granola 26–7
limes
    chocolate + lime granola 37
    granola ice cream sandwich 40
linseed: mountain muesli 54

M
mango + tahini smoothie 109
maple butter 119
    millet porridge with fresh pear +
        maple butter 63
maple syrup 10–11
    coffee, maple + walnut
        porridge 58
    maple butter 119
marmalade: oat porridge with orange,
    marmalade + thyme compote 64
mascarpone cheese: breakfast
    tiramisu 39
millet flakes
    lemon + orange millet cookies 133
    millet porridge with fresh pear +
        maple butter 63
mint: refreshing green smoothie 106
muesli 17, 43
    Bircher 17
    homemade bran flakes 52
    mountain muesli 54
    muesli + granola mix 47
    summer muesli 49
    three-grain muesli 55
    toasted buckwheat with cranberries
        + freeze-dried berries 50
    toasted lemon + ginger muesli 44
muffins
    breakfast muffins 131–2
    walnut, cranberry + courgette

muffins 134–5
mushrooms: veggie breakfast in a taco
    bowl 98–9

N
nut butter: granola ice cream
    sandwich 40
nuts, mixed
    buttermilk porridge 60
    three-grain muesli 55

O
oats
    avocado porridge with sweet
        chilli 67
    avocado with savoury granola
        crunch 35
    banana porridge with almonds +
        amaretti 68
    banana + walnut granola 36
    beetroot Bircher with apple +
        walnuts 82
    Black Forest granola with cherry
        yoghurt + cherry compote 28–9
    blackberry + apple Bircher 77
    breakfast muffins 131–2
    buttermilk porridge 60
    chocolate + lime granola 37
    cinnamon + pecan granola 25
    coconut + vanilla Bircher 87
    coffee, maple + walnut
        porridge 58
    granola ice cream sandwich 40
    green apple Bircher with
        pistachios 81
    honey + thyme granola with natural
        yoghurt + blood orange 32
    lemon + caraway granola with
        peach compote 30–1
    lemon + orange millet cookies 133
    mountain muesli 54
    muesli + granola mix 47
    oat porridge with orange,
        marmalade + thyme compote 64
    rye + oat porridge with kiwi +
        banana chips 62
    savoury porridge with lemon-

roasted fennel, beetroot chips,
    basil oil + sunflower
    'Parmesan' 70–3
spiced carrot Bircher 78
summer muesli 49
tea-soaked figs 128–9
three-grain muesli 55
toasted lemon + ginger muesli 44
oranges
    honey + thyme granola with natural
        yoghurt + blood orange 32
    lemon + orange millet cookies 133
    oat porridge with orange,
        marmalade + thyme compote 64
    orange + grapefruit Bircher with
        chilli 85
    stewed rhubarb 124

P
peach compote 30–1
peanut butter 121
pears
    chai-poached pears 120
    millet porridge with fresh pear +
        maple butter 63
pecans
    cinnamon + pecan granola 25
    granola + seed mix 127
pistachios
    green apple Bircher with
        pistachios 81
    lemon, coconut + pistachio trail
        mix 127
porridge 18, 57
    avocado porridge with sweet
        chilli 67
    banana porridge with almonds +
        amaretti 68
    buttermilk porridge 60
porridge cont.
    coffee, maple + walnut porridge 58
    millet porridge with fresh pear +
        maple butter 63
    oat porridge with orange,
        marmalade + thyme compote 64
    rye + oat porridge with kiwi +
        banana chips 62